SMART TRAINERS BRILLIANT DOGS

JANET R. LEWIS

Illustrations by Victoria A. Dale

SMART TRAINERS
BRILLIANT DOGS

by
JANET R. LEWIS

Illustrations by Victoria A. Dale

Canine Sports Productions
"Coaching the Canine Athlete" ®

Lutherville, MD 21093

Published by: Canine Sports Productions
              1810A York Rd. #360
              Lutherville, MD 21093

ISBN 1-888119-01-2

Cover Design by M. C. Zink, Timonium, MD.
Printing by BookCrafters, Chelsea, MI.

Limits of Liability and Disclaimer of Warranty:

The author and publisher shall not be liable in the event of incidental or consequential damages in connection with, or arising out of, the furnishing, performance, or use of the instructions and suggestions contained in this book.

Books are available at special discounts for bulk purchases for sales promotions, fund raising, or educational use. For details contact:

Canine Sports Productions
1810A York Rd. #360
Lutherville, MD 21093
Ph. (410) 561-1555
FAX (410) 561-1685

Printed in the United States of America

Table of Contents

About the Author

Janet Lewis has been training dogs for over 20 years. She has obtained numerous obedience and tracking titles, including three Obedience Trial Championships. Janet is in great demand for seminars because of her sense of humor and talent for teaching. Her monthly column in Front and Finish, *Gremlins*, has provided fresh training ideas to readers for over 10 years.

In her other life, Janet is an Associate Professor of Philosophy at Juniata College in Huntingdon, Pennsylvania, where she has taught philosophy and writing for the past twenty-six years. "Learning how to be an effective dog trainer — how to communicate and motivate — has improved my skill a thousandfold as a people teacher," Janet says. "Training dogs and educating humans both require an understanding of the principles of learning and a respect for the individual needs and talents of the student. Teaching and learning are the twin foundations for a partnership based on mutual trust and respect."

Foreword

I have always been a do-it-yourself kind of person. I learned how to drive a stick shift car by buying one, having a friend drive it home for me, and then lurching and stalling up and down the hills of my quiet neighborhood. I learned to cook by experimenting in the kitchen, and I could count on one hand the number of things I've made from a recipe in the last 25 years. I even represented myself when I took a terrible landlord to court to get a lien on his building so that I could recover my security deposit! So when I started training dogs, it was only natural that I wanted to design my own training program right from the beginning.

I went to obedience classes and had some wonderful instructors. But no matter how successful an instructor I found, I always found another, equally successful, instructor who used completely different methods. I wanted to know why. It wasn't enough for me to have my instructor tell me, "Do this umpteen times over the next several weeks, and then start doing that, and if you ever have any questions, don't hesitate to call!" For one thing, I was always on the phone. My dogs never seemed to go by the book. In addition, I hate being dependent upon somebody else to tell me what to do next. I am an independent kind of gal.

After a while I realized that I needed to take private lessons instead of group classes because I am the kind of student that drives everyone else crazy. I didn't just want to know what to do with the dog; I wanted to know why. I was constantly interrupting to ask, "Yes, but why did you tell Sophie to do this with her dog, while you told John to do that with his dog?" Other students' eyes would glaze over, and the instructor would offer some kindly but all too brief explanation before continuing. Private lessons allowed me to ask my many questions. But even then I often didn't get the answers I craved.

My instructors were very talented dog trainers, but it was evident early on that I was not equally gifted. Things that seemed obvious to them were far from obvious to me. Yet I enjoyed training my dogs, and I was determined not to let my lack of talent stand in my way. I have always believed that by working harder and practicing more, I could compensate for a lack of natural ability. This philosophy has gotten me far in life. (I am currently a college professor who once flunked out of school after several semesters on Strict Academic Probation.) I was sure that dog training was no different, and I vowed to learn everything I could to make up for my lack of 'dog instincts.' But I never found all the answers I needed in obedience classes or private lessons. Then I met Janet.

I didn't actually 'meet' Janet in person until I had known her for several years. I first encountered her on a computer discussion group devoted to obedience training. Right from the beginning I liked her style. She was eager to explain, to think through training problems with people, even those far less experienced than she, and she was always figuring out why something worked or didn't work. She didn't assume that those of us who were still stumbling through matches with our Novice A dogs were just dumb, despite her several Obedience Trial Champions and tournament appearances, twenty years of experience training dogs, and ten years of experience as an expert columnist in Front and Finish. She took seriously our naive questions and concerns, and considered our puzzles to be her puzzles. This was exactly what I needed. And although I didn't actually meet Janet in person until after my Novice A dog had earned her CD, Janet has been one of my most influential and important training instructors. Her thoughtful discussions of the how and why of dog training are one of the major reasons that I am now an avid participant in a number of dog sports, and did not become just another Novice A dropout.

That is why I was delighted to learn that Janet was putting into a book what she has so carefully explained to me and others via the computer and in her monthly column over the years. And unlike many other 'technical' books, this is not a book that you need to read sitting at the table with a sharp pencil in one hand and your head held, aching, in the other. This is a book with which you can curl up in your favorite chair, dogs at your feet, and something delicious to sip while you read. Prepare to meet a very personable trainer as she puzzles her way through her own and her friends' training challenges. Her stories of her dogs and her training experiences will make you feel as though you've known Janet and her dogs for years. This very experienced, knowledgable, and successful trainer not only explains the scientific foundations of dog training, but shows the places at which the science of learning theory ends and dog training becomes more like art, friendship, and teamwork than a laboratory experiment.

So get a big mug of lemonade (hot, if it is blustery outside) and a pair of comfortable slippers, curl up with a dog, and join me in this incredible journey through the mazes and labyrinths of dog training theory, guided by Janet's witty story telling and expert road maps to help us find our way. It is a journey that will make you a smarter trainer in the end. And that dog who is lounging at your side will thank you a thousand times over.

Ruth Ginzberg, Ph.D.

Acknowlegments

Writing has always been fun for me so it came as somewhat of a shock that writing a whole book was not nearly as enjoyable as I had thought it would be. One reason is because with length comes disorganization. I hadn't known that. Also, with commitment comes defensiveness. This book was my baby. No way could I believe it was less than perfect! Were it not for three special people: Ruth Ginzberg, Chris Zink, and Vicky Dale, I would have thrown in the towel — er, keyboard — long ago.

Ruth prodded me into taking my ideas and putting them into book form. She endured my less-than-grateful reactions to her relentless demands for organization and simplicity. And she kept my spirits up with her praise and encouragement. (Motivational training works on people too!) Without her, this book would not exist. If you like the book and learn from it, you her as much to her as you do to me.

Chris Zink, a professional author, editor, and fellow seminar presenter, gave me what every writer wants most — acceptance. She agreed to publish the book almost before it was written. She devoted many hours to making it reader-ready. In addition she has been a good friend and loyal defender.

Vicky Dale added a unique dimension to the book. She is not only a talented artist, she is a friend who can translate life into pen and ink. All the dogs in her sketches have personality. She used her great artistic talent and her knowledge of me and the dogs who grace these pages to transform sometimes pedantic text into pictures that both teach and entertain.

I am lucky to have three such good friends!

Thanks also go to four talented, hard-working readers — Terri Clingerman, Jane Jackson, Debbie Spence, and Gerianne Darnell — who made many suggestions on how to make the manuscript more reader-friendly, and who combed the manuscript for typos and grammatical errors.

I also owe special thanks to those who contributed photographs to the book and those posed for them. In particular, I am grateful to Sandy Roth who filled in for

Vicky as backup photographer and who dressed and posed and posed again for us to get all our pictures just right. Sandy was always sure that if we just tried it one more time we could produce the perfect picture. Thanks to her, we often did. I thank Kathy Povey, an Internet pal, who sent me many wonderful photos. The Internet can yield up amazing treasures indeed.

Finally, I would like to thank the dogs and their trainers who posed for our photos. Without them the book would not be nearly so interesting. They are: Lois Albright and her Keeshond, U-CD, U-Ch, Am/Can Ch Kee-Motion Morning Mist, Am/Can CD, Carol Crouch and her Border Collie, U-UD Tory Lane's Brandy Alexander, UDX, Can CDX, Vicky Dale and her Border Collie, U-CDX MacLeod's Star, Am/Can CDX, TD, Betsy Geertson and her Soft Coated Wheaten Terriers, U-Ch Lontree's All That Glitters Is, Am/Can CD and U-Ch Lonestar Irish Krystal O'Orion and Sandy Roth and her Welsh Springer Spaniel, Ch Auroras Gone Wythe Wynd, CGC.

Dedication — Best Pals

This part of the book is especially fun to write, especially because I write it after having finished *Smart Trainers: Brilliant Dogs*. While I have no particular desire to be famous, I relish the opportunity to give the dogs whose stories grace these pages a kind of canine immortality. It gives me comfort to know that even after I die, Lark, Amber, Kate, Coe, Mikey and the others will go on, even if their existence is hidden in some dusty and dog hair-covered corner of a dog owner's library.

Let me start at the beginning, with the most important contributors to this book, without whom it would not have been written, and with whom I have gained a share of wisdom and a measure of love I might otherwise never have had. Chronologically, this is a brief description of my most cherished companions. I will be forever grateful for the lessons they have taught me. And my love for each of them will remain undimmed forever.

Peter - My very first dog — the one who set me on my 'dog directed' course. My goodness what he taught me! He was a puppy from the first litter I whelped (my best friend's mother had allowed us to experience the wonders of birth — very liberal for the 50's). Peter was a mutt and he was, to me, the best dog in the world. He got distemper when he was a baby and I nursed him through it. Fortunately no one bothered to tell me the odds we battled through those long nights. He repaid me by being smart and loving and 100% trustworthy. Kids would come to the door and ask if Peter could come out to play. And he did, sledding down the alley behind our house, following the kids into their kitchens to share their midmorning snacks. He never met a person or a dog he didn't like and by virtue of his 'marriage' with Gina (another mutt down the street) soon invented his own little mini-breed. His efforts gave each of his early human buddies a little Peter of their own. Probably his chief claim to fame was that he survived for 16 years as a street dog — in those years runs and fenced in yards were for the rich and ostentatious. Little did we know how lucky we were.

Amber - The first dog I had as an adult. Although she was a Rough Collie she was no Lassie (nor did she much resemble Albert Payson Terhune's Lad, or Wolf, or Lady for that matter). Nonetheless I learned on her, and she is the smartest dog I have owned. Amber hated obedience (no wonder — I didn't know enough to give her a reason to like it!), but she did it anyway. She gave me my first UD, complete with my knee-shaking experience of her third leg *Stand-Stay*. I was so proud — I put her CD right up there on my office wall next to all my school diplomas. When we went to the lake in the summer Amber ate fish, whole and raw, and one day a whole bar of Irish Spring soap. She bubbled for days.

Petey - Another Rough Collie. Perhaps because he came right after Amber, and because I was not the most knowledgable of trainers, I mistakenly considered him dumb. One night, after a week of inserting the dumbbell in his mouth (including 30 or so efforts that very night), I told him, "Take it." He refused (yet again), and I clunked him over the head with it. After that Petey would never again stay in the same room with a dumbbell and his obedience career ended with a CD. Guess he taught me some stuff too!

Tiger - My last Rough Collie. Beautiful and smart and very independent — not a good combination for a performance dog. Tiger died at four years of acute pancreatitis. I learned a lot about loss from him and I still dream of trying, futilely, to find him to say good-bye. He died with a CDX, one major shy of a Championship. He loved to bark and hated the high jump and I wish I had been with him at the end.

Lark - My first Border Collie. I remember her best as a dog who chased the shadows of butterflies. She was sweet and smart and so soft. She taught me correction-free training, and she taught me how to give my soul wholly and completely to a dog. While getting her OTCh was thrilling at the time, my memories of her now are of a dog that played soccer, watched volleyball games, and was the specially appointed ball retriever of the college baseball team. She never met a sport she didn't like, and I will miss her always.

Kate - Lark's daughter and her alter ego. When I venture out-of-state, people say, "Please come and stay here, but don't bring Kate!" Kate will chase and catch anything that moves, including me if I get up suddenly to answer the telephone. She has always been drawn to small dogs and children dressed in pink. When I showed her in obedience (she was retired the day she got the third leg of her UD) friends would clear the back of the ring — small children and dogs were picked up and carried to the side. Yet at home she is the most sensitive of my dogs; when I am sad, it is Kate that knows it and snuggles her little head into me, telling me it will be okay.

Coe - Lark's son and Kate's brother. I will never have another like him. He is my cherished companion and goes to work with me every day. I never did manage to convince him that his heeling position wasn't right and it took us forever to get his OTCh. But he did it — on my birthday (never mind which one) three days after his own seventh. Maybe someday I will write a book just on him — about the day he stopped on the directed jumping to dig for groundhogs under the bar jump, or the day he picked up the correct scent article and deposited it neatly under the judge's table and then returned to work the pile for an article that was no longer there. He is my heart and soul, and I have learned to treasure every minute we have left.

Mikey - My sweet boy. He doesn't like obedience but does it because he knows it makes me happy. He is a wonderful working dog although he insists on breaking stays to visit blue Shelties (gender not important) and he is the only dog (so far) who has gotten me excused from the ring as punishment for this fetish. I don't love him as much as I should, but I do love him a whole lot. If only he didn't lick so much!

Bear - Where to begin? My bad, bold, defiant, dominant, spoiled brat. I don't think I will ever be able to totally convince her that I am leader of the pack. She failed her first novice class and heaven knows how many more she'll fail before she decides to do it my way — if indeed that ever happens. What a challenge — what fun!

Otter - Nobody likes his name but me. But he looks like one. And he has introduced me to the joys of tracking with his single minded pursuit of a smelly piece of leather. (Why do they like that?) I have no idea what kind of performance dog he will be; he is a Dog of Very Little Brain at this stage of development. He will get better — I see the joy of life shine in his eyes and he has great promise.

As I write of these dogs, I realize that one of the sorrows of growing older is that our decreasing time limits the number of dogs we have left to enjoy. I am more than happy with those I have been permitted to have and to love, but Lord, grant me time for some more!

Victoria A. Dale

Introduction — What's a Trainer to Do?

To be a truly great competition trainer — one who wins consistently, wins year after year, wins with different dogs, and wins over excellent competition — one needs great dogs (or some darn good ones), excellent natural instincts and timing, knowledge of the principles of training, and, I would argue, good luck.

But we are not all great competition dog trainers, nor do many of us aspire to that goal! We are not all equally gifted with instinct, timing, or luck, and many of us want to train a dog just to be a great companion or to exhibit a dog without the pressure to always be in the placements. This does not mean that the ordinary trainer who aspires to more personal goals cannot compete and achieve some degree of excellence. These achievements do not necessarily require private lessons with an expert trainer. Nor do they dictate that you spend your life's savings to buy a dog with an exquisite pedigree. There are other ways to do it. You can compensate for deficiencies in some areas by increasing your expertise in others.

By understanding how dogs learn, you can become a better trainer, even if your timing is not split-second, your luck is not the best, and your breed is not one of those typically associated with success in competitive performance events. That is the purpose of this book — to give all dog trainers, new and old, who are looking for a better way to train, a handle on the theory that lies behind the production of great dog/trainer teams. Although most of us will not become well known in the world of competitive dog training, all of us *can* train smarter and produce dogs that enjoy whatever skills we choose to teach them and enjoy demonstrating their skills to an appreciative audience.

A firm grounding in the principles of learning theory coupled with the partnership between you and your best canine pal can create a combination that is hard to beat in achievement or in enjoyment. This book explains the principles of learning theory that underlie all of dog training. It shows how rewards and corrections can best be applied in any training situation. It also provides many examples of dog training techniques that use those theories. This book shows you how to use learning theory to help your dog understand what you want and derive great pleasure from doing it. It teaches you how to ensure that the training/learning process does not detract from your relationship with your dog but, instead, enhances it. This book can make you not just a good animal trainer, but a skilled *teacher*.

Remember the teachers you liked best in school — the ones who honestly told you what was expected, understood when you were lost, and were willing to help and to give you a pep talk along the way? Remember how those same teachers seemed to know when you were ready to move on and be challenged, or when you were goofing off and needed to be put back

on track? Regardless of how strict those teachers were, you respected them and, if you stuck it out, you also developed a genuine affection for them.

The best teachers do not lie to their students; they don't pretend that learning is always fun and games. "Sometimes," they say, "you will have to work hard, and you will have obstacles to overcome. But if you stick it out, you will be more secure, more confident, and proud of your achievements." They explain, motivate, and insist that their pupils accomplish the task. But just as they do not lie, they do not trade in fear either. They do not threaten the student by saying, "Unless you do this, frightening and painful things will fill your life." They seem to know when to encourage, when to offer help, and when to demand that the student try harder and put a little more effort into improving and even perfecting his or her work.

Good dog trainers have the same qualities. To be truly outstanding, a dog trainer should do background research just as teachers and other educators do. They need to understand exactly how dogs learn — how and when to motivate, and how and when to demand that the dog try harder. A dog trainer needs to be part psychologist, part parent, part coach, and cheerleader, too, all wrapped up into one. Although this may seem a bit overwhelming at the beginning, if you break the process down into its separate components, each part is manageable. In fact, the various parts can be fun for you and your canine student if you give it a try.

This book begins with an examination of learning theory; in particular, a theory called **operant conditioning**. You may also have heard it referred to as **behaviorism**. Since a good trainer needs to understand the theoretical foundations that explain how our animals learn, we will start with some of the essential definitions of operant conditioning and then show you how you can apply those principles to train your own dog and teach him both to offer the behaviors you desire and to enjoy the process of learning.

Mastering learning theory, however, is only the beginning of communicating with and motivating your dog. Even though much of this book deals with theoretical principles and their applications, there is far more to training a dog than the application of any single theory of learning, regardless of how thorough it is. The good trainer must first understand the theory, then be able to translate it into practical steps to train the dog, then be flexible enough to modify the training program to the unique needs of the individual dog.

The relationships we have with our dogs are far different from those most scientists have with their experimental animals. We live with them, they're our friends and sometimes working partners — we rely on them and they on us. Because of this, training our dogs involves more than the mere application of any single scientific theory. Indeed, the field of psychology itself has already accepted other theories of learning to supplement that of operant conditioning in order to explain some ways of learning and some kinds of animal behaviors that operant conditioning cannot. This book, there-fore, discusses some ideas and concepts that do not fit neatly into the realm of behaviorism. These ideas and concepts are interspersed with the more nar-rowly defined ones used by behavior scientists. For example, although words like 'relationships' and 'choice' may not be regarded as sufficiently scientific for the laboratory, they are very important to a trainer trying to communicate with her canine friend.

This book asks that you be willing to learn the concepts of operant conditioning, but also that you not become so committed to any single theory that you are unwilling to explore alternatives or to supplement those principles with ideas from successful dog trainers and other teachers. The ultimate goal, after all, is not a degree in psychology but an approach to training that makes learning and performing in any context fun and fulfilling for both members of the partnership.

Dealing With Confusion

Recently I received a letter from a woman who signed herself simply 'An Old Time Obedience Buff.' Here, in part, is what she said. "Forty-eight years ago, when I started in obedience, everything was certainly easier. There were no 'methods' — we used whatever worked. Dog and trainer took time to evolve into a partnership. Obedience training and obedience competition were only a small part of the partnership. There wasn't a compulsion for high scores, High-in-Trials, or high anything." This writer had taken many years away from obedience to raise a family and she continued, "Now the lure of the ring is calling, and I find that competition is tougher, qualifying scores are more exacting. I'm totally confused by the myriad of training information out there and methods by the millions, workshops, seminars, videos, and books." She didn't sign her real name because, in her words, "I'd rather not be known as that Ding Bat Old Lady."

There is no need for anyone to be ashamed of being confused over the sheer quantity of information available today to any dog trainer in any performance event. Not only are there apparently conflicting methods for teaching dogs certain behaviors, there are conflicting recommendations for applying those methods to almost every training exercise. As an example, consider just the exercises for the obedience ring: there are videos on scent discrimination and on retrieves (inducive and forced), and what has been published or filmed about the mystical concept of attention could fill the library of any dog trainer all by itself!

Given the current information overload, it would be far more irrational *not* to be confused by all of the trainers and methods, ramming each other like bumper cars driven by shouting children at a carnival. The world of dog training seems to be a bewildering map of training roads that briefly intersect at some points but then go off in directions that are so widely divergent, they seem almost not to belong on the same piece of paper.

But take heart! Regardless of whether you are a beginner in dog sports, one who has returned after a long absence, or just someone who has decided to explore the art of dog training more thoroughly, the confusion is more apparent than real. It is not true that there are more methods than there were 40 years ago. It is just that trainers have become more knowledgeable about these methods — about their applications and about their inconsistencies, too. The partnership between the dog and trainer is still the key to successful training and showing. It's true that most canine sports are more competitive now. It's harder to win classes or place in tournaments, but that's partly because there is so much more good training information available.

Certainly there is conflict. Established trainers have always debated the best way to train for the long haul, and traditionalists vie with the motivational newcomers for recognition. But the debate is healthy as long as we all try to master the foundations of the theories of training — those principles of learning by which our canine buddies (and we ourselves) give some structure to our lives.

And so this book is being written for all the ding bat old ladies confused by the apparent plethora of conflicting training methodologies, for all those newcomers to obedience, equally confused, and for those in between, who want to make sense of exactly what dog training is and how it works.

The principles of operant conditioning govern much of animal learning. Although they were created and designed for working with animals in laboratory conditions, they can be translated into techniques that can help all of us train our dogs better. If we understand them and use them correctly, we can communicate to our dogs exactly what we want them to do with a far greater degree of clarity than before. This makes our training less frustrating and far more fulfilling. Operant conditioning techniques work for all levels of training and for all breeds of dogs. Understanding what motivation is and how it works, and how correctly to apply both punishment and reward can make anyone a better trainer.

Ultimately, your own training strategies will be your decision. You must decide whether you want to use only positive motivation or to use corrections as well. You must decide whether and for how long you will use food and toys in the training process, and how to train your dog in a way that is comfortable and enjoyable as well as effective. If you read this book

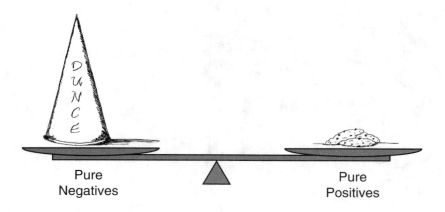

Pure Negatives — Pure Positives

carefully, you should be able to understand how and why reinforcement and punishment work, and you will be able to use that understanding to train your own dog for obedience, agility, flyball, or virtually anything. So here's to all the ding bat old ladies (and men) and to all the rest of us — dog trainers who, if we stick with it, will become better trainers, better teachers, better communicators, and better partners for our buddies at the other end of the leash. And may we have a good time doing it!

Punishment vs. Reward — An Old Controversy

Even though it seems that there are almost as many training methods as there are dogs to train, the differences among those methods are mainly superficial. In fact, most disputes about obedience training are arguments about the appropriate roles of punishment and reward in dog training. All of the arguments that deal with whether and when and how to use food and toys and other kinds of motivators, or that discuss whether and when and how to use collar pops and ear pinches and other kinds of physical compulsion are really differences of opinion on punishment and reward.

Some handlers argue that training without corrections will spoil the dog, and leave him with no real understanding of what is expected of him. They claim that without some kind of compulsion there can be no real respect between dog and trainer, no sense of duty on the dog's part to do as he is asked. There is another school of thought that holds that all forms of compulsion are unnecessarily abusive. People who consider themselves non-compulsive trainers believe that any activity that causes a handler to inflict discomfort on the dog is unjustifiable and causes needless suffering. Although the great majority of dog trainers occupy some sort of middle ground on the spectrum between those that advocate only positive rewards and those that believe only compulsion is effective, a great deal of emotional energy has gone into the reward/punishment debate.

One of the reasons that the debate continues unresolved is that much of it is based upon a misunderstanding of the efficacy of both punishment and reward in the science of operant conditioning. Trainers who endorse the primacy (or the exclusivity) of **rewards** (referred to as positive reinforcement by the founders of operant conditioning) and those who argue for the necessity of **compulsion** (also referred to as negative reinforcement or punishment) have far more in common than they realize.

Almost all dog trainers rely on the dog's ability to understand the connection between his behavior and some sort of consequence to that behavior, be it positive or negative. Only with that understanding can those consequences affect the dog's future behavior. It is those connections between

Victoria A. Dale

If you don't understand how dogs learn, you may think your dog just needs better treats or a stronger correction. In fact, it is usually not the method that is at fault, but its application.

behaviors and either reward or punishment that constitute the heart of operant conditioning. Trainers that advocate reward only, those that opt for the primacy of compulsion, and those in between all rely on the principles of behaviorism. It's just that they emphasize different aspects of that theory.

What all trainers need to understand, regardless of allegiance, is that it is not the application of punishment or reward, but the incorrect application of punishment or reinforcement that leads to unhappy dogs and frustrated trainers. Whether we choose to use positive, negative, or a mix of reinforcements, we must be sure that our buddy on the other end of the leash can identify the specific behavior for which he is being rewarded or corrected. Dogs need to understand exactly what it is that produces the cookie or the collar pop, and this must be as carefully taught as any specific physical behavior. If cookies and collar pops do not convey information to the dog about the appropriate way to act, if they don't tell him how to get the cookie or avoid the pop, then training becomes a meaningless and often frightening experience for the dog, and an exercise in frustration for the trainer.

Dogs that are trained by handlers who do not try to understand *how* their companions learn will never be able to quite master the rules of the game. Because these dogs are not sure exactly what behavior produces the cookie or exactly how they can avoid the collar pop, they become depressed. Sometimes their handlers blame the kind of reward: "He doesn't like hot dogs, but if I switch to roast beef, he'll learn better," or the kind of correction: "I must not be correcting him hard enough." Or they blame the dog, or the breed, or the stress of the sport rather than identifying the true culprit — their own lack of understanding. There is a correct way to use both positive and negative consequences to inform and motivate dogs in training. In fact, there are scientific ways to do both — ways that have produced experimentally verified results.

This book will help you understand the science of operant conditioning as it applies to dog training, and will show you how to use it to teach your dog the rules of the obedience game and enjoy playing that game. This understanding can establish and enhance the partnership that comes from having both members of the team play and enjoy the same game played by the same rules.

Each chapter of this book is a complete unit. First, a principle is introduced, defined, and explained. Then, using a specific behavior, the principle is applied in a step-by-step manner to illustrate a specific training exercise. Finally, training strategies and concepts that enhance the use of operant conditioning are provided. At the completion of each chapter, you should understand what the fundamental principle is and how to use it, and you should have other ideas for improving the teamwork between you and your dog.

1. Where to Start

The Principle:
OPERANT CONDITIONING

Training a Behavior — The Basics

In some ways training a dog is very simple. The trainer wants to teach the dog what to do and when and where to do it. A good dog trainer depends on two essential skills. She* needs to be able to both communicate (explain to the dog what to do) and to motivate (convince the dog that it is in his best interest to offer the trained behavior). These skills can be applied using the following steps.

The Training Sequence:

1. **Create** the desired behavior or cause it to occur in training situations.
2. **Define** the behavior so that the dog understands exactly what is being asked and the consequences of complying or refusing to comply.
3. **Cue** and **reinforce** the desired behavior — cause the dog to offer the behavior on a specific command and only on that command.
4. **Maintain** the behavior so that the dog continues to offer it in different places, in the presence of distractions, and even in the absence of continuous primary reinforcement.

In the case of the obedience sit, you must first create the occasion for that particular behavior to occur (Fig. 1.1), then show the dog the correct way to sit (Fig. 1.2), and teach him that it is to his advantage to offer that behavior. When you have the dog offering the correct sit, you next put that behavior on cue by assigning a specific word to it, such as, "Sit" (Fig 1.3). You then show

---

* For the sake of simplicity, the trainer will be referred to as female and the dog as male.

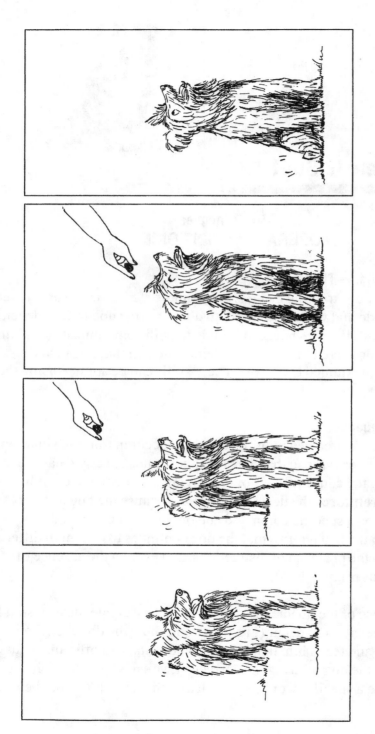

Fig. 1.1. Creating the desired behavior. In this example, the trainer is using food to lure the dog into a sit position.

Fig. 1.2. Defining the behavior. The trainer is showing the dog that jumping up is not part of a correct sit.

the dog that he needs to sit each time you give the command and that other sits will not be rewarded. Finally, you need to convince the dog that he should sit each and every time he is asked, even if sometimes there are no rewards or corrections (Fig. 1.4). We will start with a discussion of creating and defining a behavior, the beginning stages of all training. Cueing and maintaining behaviors are tasks that come later in the training process and will be discussed later in the book.

Creating and Defining a Behavior

Operant conditioning is a theory that deals with how animals learn. Its scientific foundations rest upon a law of nature called The Law of Effect, whose articulation traces back to E. L. Thorndyke, generally regarded as the first individual to research and publicize behavior theory. Thorndyke's original formulation provides the following explanation of operant conditioning:

> **The Law of Effect**
> If the occurrence of an operant is followed by the presentation of a reinforcing stimulus, then the probability of its recurrence increases.[1]

---

[1] B. Schwartz. *Psychology of Learning and Behavior*, W.W. Norton & Co. 1989, p. 22.

Fig. 1.3. Cueing and reinforcing the behavior. **a.** The trainer waits until the dog is not offering the behavior, then, **b.** gives the command. **c.** The dog sits, and, **d.** the trainer then rewards the correct behavior.

In Thorndyke's terms, an **operant** is a behavior, such as sitting, and a **reinforcing stimulus** is an event, such as being given a treat, that follows the behavior and causes it to recur. Thus, the law can be interpreted to mean that a behavior that is reinforced (i.e., produces a stimulus that is pleasurable or avoids one that is painful) is more likely to happen again. A behavior that is not reinforced is less likely to happen. The behaviors that are referred to as operants are those that are under the control of the animal. For example, your dog can decide whether he will sit or not. Hence sitting is a voluntary behavior. On the other hand, he cannot decide to elevate his temperature. That is an involuntary behavior and is therefore not subject to the Law of Effect.

Fig. 1.4. Maintaining the behavior. The dog learns to obey the command, even in the presence of distractions.

The use of food, toys, or praise is not a magic training bullet. Simply feeding a dog or playing with him will not make him learn better. Waving pieces of hot dogs in a dog's face will not help him to understand what you want him to do unless you use the food to correctly reinforce that behavior. Operant conditioning is the science that describes what a reinforcer is, and how to correctly use reinforcers to train an animal.

To teach an exercise, the trainer must cause the desired behavior to occur so that she can reinforce it and thus increase the probability of that behavior occurring again. (We will discuss ways of doing this in the next section.) Although there is much debate as to whether to use pleasurable or aversive stimuli to create and reinforce given behaviors, at this point we will concentrate on the use of **appetitive stimuli** (things a dog likes and for which he is willing to work). Appetitive stimuli are used by dog trainers who refer to themselves as motivational or food trainers. Whether they know it or not, these trainers are actually appealing to Thorndyke's Law of Effect as the basis of their training methods. They emphasize food and other pleasurable stimuli and avoid force or other negative experiences in the learning process.

After the trainer **creates** a behavior, she should reinforce it. The main thing she wants to instill in the dog's mind is a connection between a

17

pleasurable sensation and the behavior that the dog has offered. This connection must actually be taught since it is not self-evident to most dogs. Teaching the dog that there is a cause-and-effect relationship between a given behavior and the occurrence of a pleasurable sensation constitutes the **definition** of the behavior. The trainer is asking the dog to understand that there are consequences to his behaviors and that the dog himself can induce or avoid those consequences by the choices he makes.

The concept of reinforcement, which is the centerpiece of operant conditioning, explains why the dog will continue to offer the defined behavior. Reinforcement not only insures that the dog will continue to offer the behavior, it gives the dog valuable information about which behaviors are in his own best interest. This is why correct understanding of learning theory is so important for the dog trainer.

Climbing the Learning Ladder

Most dogs go through three separate steps when learning trained (i.e., artificial) behaviors. When the trainer first introduces food (or any other external stimulus), the dog has absolutely no idea why it's there (Fig. 1.5). At first he simply thinks, "Oh, she's feeding me. How nice!" He does not connect the food with the specific behavior he has offered. The food is simply seren-dipitous and it appears out of the blue for no reason at all. In the second step, the dog begins to connect food with something he does, but he responds only when the food is actually present. He has not yet grasped the concept that he has the power to produce the food by his own behavior (Fig. 1.6). It is the presence of food that causes the specific behavior that the dog offers.

Fig. 1.5. When first introduced to food, the dog does not connect the appearance of the food with his behavior.

The goal is to have the dog arrive at the third and final step — the step at which the connection between the food and the behavior becomes reversed, and the dog begins to understand that it is actually his behavior that produces the food (Fig. 1.7). The dog must realize, "Oh, she's feeding me because I sat." Dogs do not progress automatically from one step to the next, and many a good training program has floundered due to the reluctance or the inability of the trainer to move from the second to the third step. The trainer must stop enticing the dog with food, and start withholding it until after the dog offers the behavior.

Trainers need to distinguish between these three steps and move as quickly as possible from the first through the second to the third. While you cannot use food or anything else in the ring to entice your dog to offer a behavior (step two), there are certainly ways you can reinforce him for doing what you ask, such as a pat and a heartfelt, "Good boy!" at the end of an exercise successfully completed. Therefore, a sound training program uses reinforcement instead of enticement. This is critical! Certainly you want your dog to believe that all sorts of pleasurable things will happen if he comes when you call, but that is quite different from having a dog that comes only when you wave a piece of food at him.

Fig. 1.6. The dog next begins to connect food with something he is doing, but responds only when the food is present.

Applying Operant Conditioning: Teaching the Sit

Let's be honest. All dog training, whether obedience, field, agility, tracking, or whatever, can be reduced to a few simple objectives. As trainers and competitors we want our dogs to give crisp, accurate performances and to enjoy themselves while they do it. As teachers, we want to help our dogs understand what to do and to offer those behaviors with confidence, even if reinforcement is not immediately available. To achieve this, we need to have a plan of action that clearly communicates to our dogs the behaviors we wish them to perform. The following is a suggested plan for teaching something simple like the sit.

Set Precise Goals

You should have a mental picture of exactly what you want before beginning to teach it. If the dog is going to learn how to sit, it is best that he learn how to do it correctly from the start. So picture the ideal sit in your mind — one with the dog sitting squarely on both hips, front legs side by side and aligned evenly with the back legs, head up, eyes forward, spine straight. Slumping, slouching, or rolling onto one hip are not part of the ideal picture. Sitting with one front foot lifted in the air or the head cocked may look cute, but if these embroideries throw off the straightness of the sit, you should forgo them. You want the dog to maintain a happy and energetic attitude while he

Fig. 1.7. The goal is to have the dog understand
that his behavior is what produces the food.

performs this, or any, exercise. If you have trouble envisioning the ideal performance, go to a dog show and ask for directions to the obedience rings. Watch the teams work, especially those in Novice B and Open B. Chances are you will see a team that steals your heart (or knocks your socks off), and you will say, "I want my dog to look like that."

Identify the Components of the Exercise

Now that you have a picture of the ideal sit, take that picture and break it into its essential components. The best trainers break a whole exercise down into manageable chunks for the dog to master, clearly communicate what movements the dog must make in performing each chunk, and motivate the dog to joyfully offer that behavior when asked.

Training By Stages

Once you have set your goals and broken the exercise down into manageable chunks, you can start training. Begin by creating and defining the behavior.

1. Creating the Behavior

The goal here is to have the dog offer a behavior that you can **reinforce**. Since you cannot reinforce a behavior until it happens, the first step in training is to **create** the behavior. To do this, you can either cause your dog to exhibit the desired behavior, or you can wait for him to offer it naturally so that it can be reinforced. Your strategy depends on the behavior you have chosen. To train the sit, you could just wait for the dog to sit all by himself and then reinforce the action. But most people are not observant enough and don't spend enough time with their dogs to reinforce a sit each and every time the dog offers one. In addition, unless your timing is perfect, you may end up reinforcing the dog for the wrong behavior. For example, if his sit is just a first stage before lying down, you must reward him before he begins to lie down. In addition, the dog's sit position may not be correct (e.g., he may be slouched over on one hip). It is more difficult and time consuming to retrain an incorrect position than to teach the position correctly in the first place.

It is better to set up a situation in which the dog is induced to assume the correct position. One way to do this is to use compulsion — to physically induce the dog to sit (Fig. 1.8). This is a common way to teach the exercise. Take the dog's collar and pull slowly upward and backward while pressing down on the rump where the tail joins the body.

There is a second, entirely positive, alternative that doesn't use physical compulsion. Lure the dog into a sit by positioning food slightly above his head and slowly moving it back, causing the dog to raise his head and lower his rear in order to follow the food (Fig. 1.9). When the dog has assumed the correct position, he is given the food and is thus reinforced for the correct sit. Food is often used to lure the animal into assuming simple positions like the sit. Food creates an initially positive association with training and is therefore preferred by many trainers. It's especially useful for training puppies.

There is also a middle-of-the-road method. Use the food as a lure to cause the dog to raise his head and, at the same time, hold the collar gently, preventing him from moving forward or jumping up for the food (Fig. 1.10). As soon as the dog sits, give the food as a reinforcer. Dogs trained in this way will be accustomed to being both compelled and lured into a desired behavior and then rewarded for that behavior. This combination of compulsion and positive reinforcement is favored by many trainers.

There are advantages and disadvantages of each of these methods for creating a behavior. Compelled behaviors have the advantage of being more accurate at the beginning. The handler can physically place the dog in precisely the correct position. In addition, training by compulsion progresses more rapidly in the beginning. It may take a long time to lure or wait for behaviors to naturally occur at a time when the trainer is able to reinforce them. Further, dogs trained using compulsion are not distracted by the presence of the food. (For example, a dog may leap and bite at the food instead of assuming the desired sit position).

A disadvantage of compulsion is that there's a natural tendency for dogs to resist pressure. Pulling or pushing a dog in one direction will often cause him to exert effort in the opposite direction. Unless the handler uses the most effective leverage point to create the sit, she may find herself in a pushing contest with the dog. In addition, if the pressure is incorrectly applied, such as by pushing down on the back, the dog may actually be injured by the pressure. Further, dogs learn to tolerate more and more force, and the trainer may end up having to exert much more effort (and perhaps pain) to elicit the correct behavior. Finally, some dogs are frightened by any sort of physical compulsion. Using compulsion at the onset of training could create powerful negative associations with training, and the trainer may find that her dog runs and hides each time she picks up the collar and leash. He might never learn to enjoy the exercises that triggered those earlier negative associations.

Fig. 1.8. The trainer is pulling up on the dog's collar and pressing in on his rear legs to induce him to sit.

23

Fig. 1.9. The dog is lured into a sit by positioning food above his head, causing him to raise his head and lower his rear.

Fig. 1.10. The food is used as a lure to cause the dog to raise his head, and gentle use of the collar keeps him from moving forward or jumping up.

One of the advantages of luring an animal into offering a behavior or letting the behavior occur naturally is that the dog *voluntarily* offers the behavior. Research has shown that animals learn more quickly when they control their body positions themselves. Indeed, some dogs seem to learn nothing about positioning themselves if their handlers constantly place them in the desired position. They seem to believe that 'sit' means that the handler pulls up and pushes down, and they just go with the flow.

On the other hand, to lure the dog into the correct position requires good timing on the part of the trainer and the ability to position the food in exactly the right place. A lure inappropriately placed or a treat inappropriately timed can reinforce an incorrect position and confuse the dog. Some trainers may do more harm than good by using lures for certain behaviors. For example, food held too high above a dog's head can cause him to jump up rather than sit, and food held too far forward may cause him to step forward.

If the trainer is careful and understands how positive experiences motivate a dog, the use of food or other appealing objects can create a positive attitude towards training. This is the main reason that luring and gentle positioning accompanied by immediate positive reinforcement is the most desirable method for creating behaviors in most beginner dogs and all puppies.

2. Defining the Behavior

Once the behavior has been created, the trainer must move immediately from luring to reinforcing the behavior. Although luring and reinforcing both involve the use of food, there is a tremendous difference between them, and many a training program has failed because the trainer did not understand that difference. Unless you understand the difference between luring and reinforcing, you risk producing a dog that is incapable of offering any trained behaviors unless food is present. You must help the dog understand that there is a specific connection between his behavior and the reinforcement.

Luring vs. Reinforcing

Luring: The dog is offering the behavior when food is present (whether the food is visible or not).

Reinforcing: The dog offers the behavior when food is not present. He is concentrating on what to do to get the food.

The Pitfalls of Luring

(A story to demonstrate that not all food training is equal.)

I was invited by a kennel club in a nearby city to attend one of their meetings and give a talk on the proper uses of food in training. The club president offered to meet me at the outskirts of the city so that I could follow her to the clubhouse. Since I was traveling alone and would be arriving at dusk in the midst of rush hour traffic, I gratefully accepted. She met me at a thruway exit. I noted the make of her car and its license number, and away we went. It required all of my concentration to follow her for five miles in heavy traffic, but we arrived at the meeting on time. After my talk, I asked for directions back to the thruway since the president had to stay and conduct the business meeting. She said, "You should have no trouble getting back to the thruway — just go back the way we came."

I got lost before the end of the first block! I had no idea of "the way we came." Every ounce of my concentration had been focused on following the other car. I had paid no attention at all to turns, street signs, or landmarks. Finding my way back was like trying to find my way through a maze.

My successful trip into the city and my equally unsuccessful attempt to leave it illustrate both the benefits and the pitfalls of luring. I was easily lured to the meeting site, but once the lure was removed, I was unable to find my way out. I had learned nothing.

The Trap

Once your dog moves past the first step in the learning process and realizes that food is present for a reason, he will begin to concentrate on its presence, and use it as a guide for correct behavior. But he is still essentially a passive participant in the learning process. When you lure your dog into a sit and keep him there by allowing him to nibble on a piece of food, all that you have taught him is to hold still in a sitting position with his head up and take the treat. This is a very effective and pleasant way to cause the dog to assume the correct position. You have indeed **created** the desired behavior by teaching the dog to follow food. However, unless you move from luring to reinforcing, you have not **defined** the exercise to the dog. He has been taught to follow food, but has not been taught what sitting is. Just because a dog sits in response to food held over his head does not mean that he understands the sit command (Fig. 1.11), nor does it mean that he will sit in response to that command if food is not present.

Fig. 1.11. If you only lure, the dog never truly learns the behavior.
He depends on the presence of the lure to tell him what to do.

In fact, the dog has no more learned what you set out to teach him than
I had learned to navigate the streets of a strange city by following a friend's
car. When a lure is present, every bit of attention is focused on it. Neither dog
nor driver is actually thinking about what they are doing or where they are
going. Nothing is being learned, even though the presence of the lure makes it
appear that way.

The dog has made progress by the time he reaches this stage and he
knows there is a connection between the food and his behavior. However, he
still needs to understand that if he sits in response to a cue word (command),
he will be rewarded. His dependency on the presence of something external
(whether it be a gentle tap on the butt or a piece of cheese over the nose)
needs to be gradually decreased. He must grasp the idea that he has the power
to control the consequences of his actions. This is the transition to cueing,
where the dog figures out that he should offer the behavior on command.

The pitfall of luring is the deceptive picture that it paints. Your dog can
look so good when food is present as a lure. Together, you have created the
ideal picture. Training buddies are greatly impressed. "Wow, I would never
have thought you'd get him to work that well so quickly!" It looks as though
the dog truly understands what is expected of him when the food is there, just
as it looked like I knew my way through the city as long as the luring car was

Fig. 1.12. The pitfall of luring is that once the
food is removed, the performance deteriorates.

in front of me. But the picture is false because if the lure is taken away, the
performance evaporates (Fig. 1.12).

The beauty of this false picture is addictive. The performance looks so
good with food present that the trainer finds it difficult to do without the food.
If the trainer suddenly removes the food without a careful transition from food
to no food, the performance deteriorates. When the food reappears, the performance returns. Thus, the trainer is reinforced for keeping food in the picture.

Many trainers who believe that food must be used all the time when
the dog is in the process of learning a behavior do not bother to teach the dog
to perform the behavior without food. The food works so well that they hope
to keep the dog believing that there will always be food. When they compete,
they try to trick the dog into believing that food might appear at any second if
he performs well. They do not believe that the dog can learn to work well
without food. Or perhaps they think that it's not necessary for the dog to learn
to work without food. What many of them do not understand is that the continuous presence of the food as a lure prevents the dog from moving beyond
the early stages of training because dog *and* handler are being taught to depend on external help to accomplish the tasks.

How to Make the Transition Clear

You can use the 'watch' exercise to determine whether your dog is
responding to food as a lure or as a reinforcer. First, teach your dog to look at

your face by luring his gaze upwards with a piece of food slowly moved from in front of his nose to your face. Next, place the food between your lips so that it is visible to the dog. When the dog looks up at your face, say, "Good watch" and give him the food. Your dog will quickly learn that if he looks at your face, he will get the food. But is he looking at your face or at the food? Will he look at your face if the food is not visible between your lips?

Now work on the transition to no food. Gradually make the food less visible by moving it farther into your mouth. Usually the dog's attention remains constant. Even if he cannot see the food, he knows (or thinks he knows) that the food is there. As long as the dog is responding to the presence of food (even if that presence is imagined), he is still at the luring stage. What happens when the food is removed from the mouth and held in your hand?

At first, your dog will transfer his attention from your face to your hand, even though the 'watch' command is given. He may even nuzzle your hand to see if he can persuade you to give him the treat. But you should not give the treat until he looks away from your hand and back at your face. When that happens, praise and feed him immediately. You are showing him that even if food is present, he cannot earn it simply by looking at it. He must offer you a behavior that takes his attention away from the food to get it. Now the food is being used not as a lure, but as a reinforcer. The process is complete when you can say, "Watch," and the dog transfers his attention away from any distraction to your face, even if the food is not present.

This transition is not a natural one for the dog. Indeed, some trainers believe that because dogs become so dependent upon the presence of food, its presence detracts from the dog's ability to learn new behaviors. They are suspicious of the addictive properties of food and want their dogs to work because they are told to work, not just for the opportunity to get a cookie.

Moving from luring to reinforcing does not just happen. The dog needs to be taught that even if the food is hidden, he can make it reappear. This lesson must be carefully planned. Imagine what would have happened to me if my city guide had arbitrarily decided that I had followed her long enough and that it was time now for me to make it on my own. Not only would I have been hopelessly lost, I would have lost confidence in my ability to find my way around, and I would have become annoyed with my friend. It would take a while before I trusted anyone to lead me around again.

Most competitive dog sports demand that the dog perform without food. The dog therefore must reach this third step in the learning process. He must be able to offer the behavior on command, without food or toys to cause the behavior or to motivate him to do it. And he must understand that there will be times when he will be asked to perform knowing very well that there is no immediate reinforcement.

The Fallacy of the False Cause

Many trainers, after watching their dogs perform satisfactorily again and again in the presence of food, believe that since the dog is performing the behavior correctly, there is no longer any need for food. So they simply take the food away. Their reasoning is based on two false assumptions: first, that food itself can cause understanding, and second, that once the dog has learned the behavior, the food is no longer necessary. The first mistake prevents the trainer from making the transition from luring to reinforcing. The second prevents her from finding creative and motivational techniques for using food or other positive reinforcers in ways that are allowed at performance events.

We already know that luring does not contribute to learning. Therefore, it is logical to expect that when the food is removed without transitions, performance will deteriorate almost immediately. Trainers who operate on the above assumptions now decide that the dog really does not understand what is expected and go back to offering food. And the food looks as though it has helped because the dog, his training aid restored, again offers the desired behavior. The trainer is convinced that the dog still needs the food because he is still in the process of learning the behavior. Food used in this fashion can actually be destructive to a training program. It can prevent the dog from learning on his own because he is never encouraged to do anything more than respond to an external guide. He never needs to think on his own or to act on his own because the food is always there to show him what to do.

Trainers who don't progress beyond using food as a lure frequently give it up altogether, often with a degree of righteous indignation, saying, "I knew food training was nothing more than a fad." Experienced dog trainers who have switched to food but have not devoted specific attention to the transition period usually become equally disillusioned. And those who oppose food in training nod their heads and wisely proclaim the superiority of their own non food-based method.

Making the Transition

If food (or other appealing stimulus) is to be effective long-term, you must move from using it as a lure to using it as reinforcement. The dog will still be working for the food, but food need not be present for the behavior to occur. Simply stated, the food is presented after the behavior rather than before.

Teaching the Transitions

I recommend that you try to get all food off your person as soon as possible. I carry food in plastic bags in my training bag which, for a beginning dog, is always close to where I train. When the dog gives me a behavior I want to reinforce, I release him and run with him to the training bag. I do not want him to form an association between the presence of food on my body and correct behaviors. Although it may seem easier to keep food in a pocket or in a bait bag, this presents a very different picture than the dog will see during competition. It is a costly mistake to teach your dog that you cannot reinforce him unless you are carrying food on your body.

Remember, reinforcement *follows* the performance of the desired behavior. When the dog performs exactly as you desire, the food is offered immediately. The reinforcement serves a double purpose here: it tells the dog the behavior was correct and it increases the probability he will offer that behavior again. Now the dog begins to understand that his behavior results in a reward and that he may need to perform the behavior in the absence of food (Fig. 1.13). He has faith that he will eventually be reinforced, but he is not dependent on the presence of food in order to offer the behavior on his own.

It is essential to move quickly from luring to reinforcing. Only when the dog offers the behavior in the absence of food can you be sure that the dog really understands. Remember that the competition obedience dog must be able to perform an entire routine without food. Dogs that are dependent on the presence of food to perform are incapable of such routines.

More important, dogs that cannot offer behaviors in the absence of some external lure do not understand their trainer's commands and, therefore, are not trained at all!

Fig. 1.13. The dog truly understands the exercise only when he is able to offer the behavior in the absence of the reinforcer.

2. Accentuate the Positive

The Principle:
REINFORCEMENT

The nature of reinforcement and its timing and delivery are essential for a dog trainer to master. If you understand exactly what reinforcers are and how they work, you can communicate to your dog what you want and reward him once he's done it. A properly timed reinforcer tells your dog, "Right on!" and makes it worth his while to be right the next time, too.

Reinforcement — A Primer

Reinforcement is any response by the trainer to a dog's voluntary behavior that *increases* the probability that the behavior will be offered again. If you give your dog a sirloin steak after he comes to you on command, you make it more likely that he will come to you the next time you call. The sirloin reinforces the recall. It is not the fact that the dog likes the steak that makes it reinforcing, it is the fact that the steak increases the probability of the dog responding to your command the next time. Dogs are like people. Although we are fond of many things, we are not willing to work for all of them. Something is reinforcing only if we are willing to work to obtain it.

For example, my dog Bear likes to be stroked very much indeed. She indicates this by leaning on me and looking remarkably content whenever I pet her. But this physical interaction is not always sufficient for her to race across the room when I call her. On the other hand, the prospect of a spirited game of tug is worth a very brisk recall. Although Bear likes both being stroked and being played with, only the play is reinforcing because she is willing to work to obtain it.

How Reinforcement Works

Sometimes it's hard to understand what dogs find reinforcing or why. There also may be confusion over whether it is the object or the activity associated with the object that the animal works to obtain. Is it food and toys, or is it eating and playing that dogs find so reinforcing? Regardless, the trainer should be aware that no objects and no activities are reinforcing all of the time. Reinforcement is always relative to the dog's instincts, his personality, his physical condition, and the environment.

Psychologist David Premack argued that no activity was absolutely reinforcing (i.e., reinforcing all the time). He determined that whether or not something was reinforcing was dependent upon its relevance to the behavior it was intended to reinforce.

Premack's Principle

The opportunity to engage in behavior A will reinforce behavior B only if the animal prefers to engage in behavior A more frequently than behavior B.

Therefore, the only way to determine which activity (e.g., eating) would reinforce another activity (e.g., jumping) would be to examine the relative frequencies of both eating and jumping. If the dog chose to eat more frequently than it chose to jump, then eating would reinforce jumping. If, on the other hand, the dog chose jumping over eating, then eating would not be reinforcing to jumping.

My mother used to say that my brother would rather sleep than eat. Premack's Principle tells us that it would have been useless for my mother to use food to reinforce nap time ("Here, Jimmy, have a cookie for taking your nap.") But she could have used the opportunity to sleep to reinforce picky eating ("If you eat all your lunch, you can have a nice long nap.") For a child who enjoyed food immensely and was reluctant to take naps, the reinforcements would be exactly the reverse.

Let's say you have a fanatic retriever who chases and carries everything he can. If he engages in retrieving activity more frequently than eating, food cannot be used to reinforce retrieving since that dog will not retrieve in order to obtain food. Retrieving is largely an instinctive response, and dogs with abundant retrieving instinct do not need to be reinforced by anything at all outside of the opportunity to retrieve. The wise trainer will use that desire to retrieve to reinforce other exercises. My dogs all love to retrieve the glove in the obedience *Directed Retrieve* exercise. Since getting the glove is the essential part of the exercise, I use the retrieve to reinforce the dog for correctly identifying the glove that I select. If the dog looks at the correct glove, I reinforce that by giving him the opportunity to retrieve the glove. How nice to be able to use the exercise itself as a reinforcer!

On the other hand, if a dog is not so enamored of retrieving, the opportunity to do so will have no reinforcing effect. In fact, dogs that are not interested in retrieving the glove may be discouraged from looking at the correct one because they then have to go and get it. A good trainer can use that to her advantage, too. For example, my collie Amber hated to retrieve, but she learned the obedience *Scent Discrimination* exercise quickly, since if she brought the correct article back, I did not send her to search for another. The quicker she was right, the less she had to retrieve.

It's not enough, therefore, to know what your dog does and doesn't like. You also must determine the order of his preferences. If he likes tug-of-war more than chasing a ball, you can use the tug game to reinforce the retrieve. On the other hand, if he prefers ball chasing, then you can use that to reinforce other activities he likes less. Sometimes dogs will perform an exercise correctly because it means that they can stop (like Amber and the scent articles). Others perform correctly because it gives them the opportunity to perform again. You need to figure out which kind of dog you have!

Positive Reinforcement

Animal trainers divide reinforcers into four categories: positive and negative, primary and secondary. When classifying reinforcements as positive or negative, it is best to think of the terms as mathematical rather than emotional. A reinforcer is **positive** if it is added to the situation and **negative** if it is removed. When we positively reinforce, we add something to the situation that the dog will work to obtain. When we negatively reinforce, we remove something the dog will work to avoid.

An **appetitive stimulus** is something that the dog will work to obtain. It is appetitive because it appeals so strongly to the dog's appetite or natural desires that the dog will be willing to offer a behavior to get it. It is a stimulus because it stimulates the dog to action. Most dog trainers use food and toys because food appeals to dogs' desire to eat and toys to their desire to play. The strengths of appetitive stimuli are relative — they vary according to the dog's preferences, his instincts, and his present condition. A natural retriever may be reinforced by chasing a tennis ball over and over, whereas a dog that was not bred for high chase instinct or prey drive may have no desire to carry a smelly old ball. Some dogs are not particularly interested in food. They will eat if you offer them food, but they won't get up to walk across the room for a piece of hot dog. For these dogs, food is not sufficiently appetitive to be reinforcing. It follows, therefore, that play would not reinforce a tired dog, nor is food something an ill dog would work to obtain. It is important that you determine exactly what your dog finds stimulating enough to work for and use those reinforcers if at all possible. Even more important, you should work hard to establish yourself — your voice, your touch, your attention, your approval, your overall presence — as the main reinforcer (Fig. 2.1).

Creating Reinforcers

Even though many activities are naturally desirable to animals, you can actively work to make the stimulus or activity more or less appetitive. Many trainers believe that by restricting access to an activity, it becomes more desirable. The expression, "Why buy the cow if you can get the milk for free?" holds true for dogs, too. If I praise, stroke, and feed my dog each time he nuzzles me, why should he work for these things? Although this may seem to be common sense, it does have some interesting applications in training.

Many trainers advocate training the dog when he is lonely and bored (Fig. 2.2). By depriving the dog of their company for a period of time, their resumed presence will be more interesting to the dog, and he will be more

Fig. 2.1. You should be your dog's main reinforcer.

likely to work to obtain their attention. Others restrict access to food or to play prior to training on the theory that a hungry dog will find food more reinforcing than a full one, and that an energetic dog will find play more reinforcing than a tired one. This is not to say that you should deprive your dog of his dinner or of your company if you want him to obtain obedience or agility titles. However, you do need to consciously use the training sessions to provide the dog with an opportunity to engage in activities he enjoys with the person he most enjoys — and this should be you. Try to offer those objects or activities that are most reinforcing to your dog only in the context of training or competition. And try to make yourself the most desirable presence at those times.

On the other hand, if you allow your dog unlimited access to your reinforcers (Fig. 2.3), they will be much less reinforcing in the training session. By all means, play with your dog outside of the training area, but don't play with him so much that the play associated with training becomes mundane. If he enjoys some games more than others, play those games with him only during training sessions.

Fig. 2.2. If you deprive your dog of your company for a period of time before your training session, it will help him focus on you.

Fig. 2.3. Your reinforcers will be less effective in training sessions if you allow your dog unlimited access to them at other times.

Since you intend to make yourself the main reinforcer, be sure that during the training sessions your dog is the exclusive object of your attention. You should permit no interruptions for phone calls or for chatting with a passing neighbor. This is not to say that the only time you are to pay attention to your dog is during training. But you should try to make the quality of that training attention very special indeed (Fig. 2.4). This is easier in multi-dog or multi-person households in which the dog must share the trainer's affection and attention with others. If you have only one dog, or if you are the only person in your home, you may have to work a little harder. I try to initiate training sessions immediately after I have been concentrating on something other than the dogs, such as a session in front of the computer or a long, chatty telephone call. When I hang up, I look at my dog and say, "Oh, you're here! How would you like to go out and practice?" Usually this question is met with a wild and enthusiastic response.

Negative Reinforcement

Just as positive reinforcement occurs when an appetitive stimulus is *added* to the situation, negative reinforcement occurs when an aversive stimulus is *removed* from the situation. **Aversive stimuli** are events in the environment that animals find distasteful, like the heat of the sun on a summer's day or loud noises — things of which an animal is afraid or which cause him physical discomfort. When a dog's action successfully removes an aversive stimulus, the dog is negatively reinforced (i.e., he is more likely to perform the same action again because of the removal of the discomfort). Remember, the removal of the stimulus is reinforcing only if the probability of the dog offering the same avoidance behavior in the future is increased.

I use a form of mild negative reinforcement to teach my dogs to walk on a loose lead. If the dog pulls too far out ahead of me, the leash tightens and creates the unpleasant sensation of the collar pulling against his neck. As soon as I feel the leash tighten, I stop and wait. Now two unpleasant things have happened: the collar is uncomfortably tight, and the dog cannot move forward on the walk he wants so badly. If the dog takes a step backwards, two things happen: the pressure of the leash is released, and I step forward to continue the walk. In effect, the dog has removed two aversive stimuli from the environment, both the unpleasant collar pressure and the cessation of forward motion. He is reinforced to offer the behavior that keeps the leash loose the next time. Thus, the dog is **reinforced** to walk on a loose leash, and the

Fig. 2.4. Work hard to make your training great fun!

reinforcement is **negative** in the sense that the aversive stimulus has been removed from the environment.

Like appetitive stimuli, aversive ones are relative to the dog's situation. For example, dogs are normally very uncomfortable when they see their owner approaching in anger. But some get so anxious about being left alone on the obedience stay exercises that they actually prefer the return of an angry owner bent on correction to the terrors of being deserted. The trainer may view the correction she has returned to administer as aversive, but the dog may prefer even negative attention to no attention at all. Thus, dogs rank aversive stimuli just as they do appetitive ones.

It is essential that you learn what your dog is willing to work to avoid. Be careful not to substitute your preferences for those of your dog. Some things that we find extremely aversive are very appetitive to our dogs (like all those foul-smelling things our dogs love to roll in). Remember, too, that the effectiveness of an aversive stimulus is not always commensurate with what we perceive as the degree of discomfort. If a little spritz of water from a spray bottle will stop your dog from barking, why get an electronic bark collar?

Negative and positive reinforcers work in opposite ways. Just as a dog will work to obtain an appetitive stimulus, so he will work to avoid or eliminate an aversive one. When the dog takes action to avoid something that causes discomfort, he is being negatively reinforced by the removal of the unpleasant object. The behavior is reinforced because the probability of the behavior being offered again is increased.

Although some people regard the application of aversives in any situation as cruel, if you think of the application of an aversive stimulus as a means of communication rather than as a device calculated to cause pain, negative reinforcement makes sense. Remember, reinforcement ought to contribute to an animal's understanding of the situation. It should improve the dog's ability to offer rewardable behaviors in the future. You may have used a clicker to play a game similar to the old children's game, in which the words 'hot' or 'cold' were used to direct a child to an object. The child was told she was hot when she was close to the object and cold if she moved away. Even though it is true that the word 'cold' carries a negative meaning to the players and is a word the game tells them to avoid, the vast majority of players prefer being told they are wrong to being told nothing at all. Even though such words have negative meanings, they are valuable because of the information they supply. It is true that none of us likes bad news, but if that news provides information to make sure similar events never happen again, while the news may be negative, it's still valuable.

A chocaholic friend of mine hates to do the dishes. But she has set a rule for herself: no dishes, no chocolate cake. As soon as she washes the dishes, puts them away, and cleans the counter, she sits down and has a big piece of chocolate cake (Fig. 2.5). This is positive because the opportunity to eat the cake is added to the situation, and reinforcement because it increases the probability that the next time there are dirty dishes and a chocolate dessert, she will be more likely to do the dishes quickly.

Unfortunately, chocolate cakes are not always available, so she has another rule. As soon as dinner is finished, she sets a loud timer and carries it around with her. She finds the constant ticking annoying, and it prevents her from concentrating on her favorite book or television show. When the dishes have been done, she turns it off (Fig. 2.6). The ticking is a negative that she seeks to remove. That negative is reinforcing because she is much more likely to do the dishes immediately after dinner the next time and thus avoid the annoying ticking of the timer. Of course, eating the cake and removing the sound is a more powerful combination than either one alone!

From The Dog's Point of View

One of the first things most of us teach our dogs is to sit on command. To teach the sit using positive reinforcement, you might take a piece of chicken and, holding it over your dog's nose, move it slowly backwards and say, "Sit." As soon as his little rump hits the floor, you would say, "Good sit," and give him the food. This is positive because the opportunity to eat the chicken is added to the situation, and reinforcing because, if he likes the chicken enough to work for it, he will be more likely to sit the next time.

Fig. 2.5. An example of positive reinforcement. Once the dishes are done, you can have a piece of chocolate cake.

41

Fig. 2.6. Negative and positive reinforcement. When the dishes have been washed, the timer (negative) is turned off, and the cake (positive) is eaten.

Now you want to teach him to lie down. You put a leash on his collar and exert pressure toward the ground by pushing the leash down with your foot and saying, "Down." The pup figures out that he can release the pressure by lying down and does so. This is negative in that he has released the pressure of the leash (removed an aversive from the situation) and reinforcing in that he will be likely to try to avoid that pressure by lying down the next time. If you were to also give him a piece of chicken after he lay down, you would be using both negative and positive reinforcers for the same exercise.

Note that dogs do not automatically know that the stimuli are causally connected to their behavior. In the first stage of learning, the dog thinks that the appearance of food has nothing to do with his behavior. Therefore, it is critical that you teach the dog how to obtain or remove the stimuli, particularly if you choose to apply an aversive during early training. For an aversive stimulus to work correctly, to be non-abusive and reinforcing, the dog must know how to turn off or escape from the aversive stimulus. For example, initially you may help a puppy to lie down if he struggles at the pressure of the leash. It may be necessary to show him that, by lying down, he can release the pressure. Simply pulling on his neck won't help until he understands the relationship between his actions and the leash pressure.

An Important Reminder:
Whether a stimulus is positive or negative, what makes it reinforcing and effective in training) is not whether the dog likes or dislikes it, but

whether its *addition* to, or its *removal* from the environment brings about an increase in the behavior it is intended to reinforce.

Primary Reinforcers

A stimulus is a **primary** reinforcer if the dog does not have to be taught to obtain or avoid it. In most cases, primary reinforcers satisfy an animal's biological needs (such as food or water), or their removal (e.g., pain or cold) ensures its survival. Activities that appeal to a dog's natural instincts can also function as primary reinforcers. For instance, ball chasing satisfies the prey or chase instinct of many dogs. Primary reinforcers are also called **unconditioned reinforcers** since the animal need not be conditioned or taught to find them appetitive or aversive.

Primary reinforcers vary from dog to dog and change in both nature and degree because dogs differ in what they prefer. The opportunity to be squirted with a hose may be immensely satisfying to a Labrador Retriever, yet terribly aversive to a Basenji. Experienced trackers have long known that, for some dogs, the article at the end of the track is sufficient incentive to follow the scent, while for others, the track itself reinforces the activity so strongly that these dogs must be taught to stop and indicate the article. Still other dogs are reinforced neither by finding the article nor by following the track. These dogs can still be induced to track by the presence of food either on the track or the article at the end.

Toys and Games

Food is the most commonly used primary reinforcer. Many people use food because it has some advantages over other external sources of reinforcement. The dog can quickly consume food and get back to work, and most dogs prefer eating to almost any other activity. But toys can also be valuable in the training program, and games that serve to focus the dog's attention on the trainer are invaluable because clever trainers can devise ways to play subtle versions of training games in the ring quite legally.

There are also problems with using toys and games. If used incorrectly, they can disrupt a training session or impair the relationship between dog and trainer. For example, many people who use a toy as a reinforcer must take time out from training so the dog can play. Some toys may become so attractive to the dog that his attention is diverted from both the task at hand

and from the trainer. If toys are to be used, the trainer must know how to use them to focus the dog's attention on the task.

Some dogs can become so fixated on toys that it takes a considerable amount of time for the trainer to get the toy back. The process of making the dog give up the toy can impair rather than enhance the training relationship. The more we use toys, especially if our use of them serves to direct the dog's attention away from us, the more distractible a dog may become. I know a dog that races for the training bag the moment the trainer releases him from command. He roots frantically in the bag for a favorite toy, oblivious to the presence of the trainer. Imagine how distracted he will be in the performance ring if a person outside the ring is using a toy or the show photographer in the next ring is throwing squeaky toys to attract the attention of his subjects.

Nevertheless, if used correctly, toys can have great value. If you want to throw a toy as a reinforcer, you should keep another toy or two on your person. A dog taught to play with toys correctly knows that, after he retrieves the toy, there is another toy waiting for him if he races back to the trainer. This way the dog can be reinforced with an exercise that appeals to his chase instinct and then redirected to his trainer. And, because he is given another toy on his return, the trainer need not pry the retrieved toy from the dog's mouth after his return.

There are occasions, such as the obedience *Broad Jump* exercise, in which the dog's attention should be directed away from you, and toys work well for that, too. To perform this exercise, the dog must pay attention to the jump. A dog who can only look at his trainer's face cannot correctly judge how to clear the jump. Inexperienced dogs often go straight to the trainer, cut the corner of the jump, or land on the last board when commanded to jump because they are too focused on the trainer. The trainer should teach the dog not only to look at the jump, but to actually take a stride or two past it after landing. A toy placed out in front of the jump and, in the course of training, gradually hidden under a mat or in the grass, helps define a point of focus for the dog (Fig. 2.7). However, the wise trainer holds another toy or goodie so that, when the dog gets the first toy, he is immediately motivated to take it to his handler to exchange for the second. Toys can also be used beneficially in the *Directed Jumping* exercise to draw the dog's attention away from the handler's face and to the hand holding the toy, a hand which is conveniently located on the end of the arm that is signalling which jump to take.

Kathy Povey

Fig. 2.7. A toy is placed out in front of the broad jump to help the dog focus ahead rather than on the trainer. When the dog sits in front, the handler exchanges the retrieved toy for another.

Some dogs are not particularly motivated by treats, no matter how tasty. In this case, the trainer must find something that is more reinforcing. Understandably, most trainers refuse to starve their dogs just so they will be hungry enough to be reinforced by food in training sessions. So if food is not effective and toys are only of limited use, what else is there?

My dog, Bear, taught me a valuable lesson about food. Although she likes food, and will eat it when it's offered, she does not do so with any great enthusiasm. The more I watched her, the clearer it became that she was not working for the food even though she would accept it politely after the exercise. What Bear seemed to find exciting was the *activity* inherent in the obedience exercises. So I decided to incorporate games that could be played either in the middle of an exercise, such as after a particularly nice about turn while heeling, or between the exercises themselves.

One of Bear's favorite games is to play with a tug toy. So I taught her to play tug with the leash, first by giving her a release command, "Okay, get it!" which released her to leap up and grab the leash. (I also taught her a stop command, very necessary for a dog that tends to get overexcited.) As soon as

Fig. 2.8. A quick game of tug can serve as a great stress release.

Bear grabs the leash, we engage in a short, spirited game of tug. This serves several functions. When we play tug prior to competition, the game gets her revved for action, and it is also a great stress releaser (Fig. 2.8). I can use it in a training session to immediately reinforce any kind of on-leash behavior she offers. Although the leash is something like a toy, the leash itself is not the focus of primary reinforcement — the activity with me is. She can't play tug without me on the other end. This game keeps Bear focused on me. It can easily be played as we heel from one exercise to another or from one training area to another. The leash is always there when I train. If it's not on the dog, I keep it around my neck so I need not fumble to get it out and thus compromise the timing of the reinforcement.

Another of Bear's favorites is the game of two hoses. It involves two pieces of hose (obtained and cut to order at any auto supply store, or cut from a garden hose) long enough for the dog to grip the middle and for the trainer to hold at the ends. I hide a piece of the hose under my left arm and when Bear does a wonderful finish or heels well, I simply lift my arm and let the hose drop. We can play tug at this point, or I can throw one hose and, when she returns with it, throw the other (Fig. 2.9). This keeps her focused on me as the source of reinforcement and of sudden fun. If your dog isn't hungry, or is just plain bored with hot dogs, games like this add a wonderful kind of focused variety. With both of these games, it's very easy to fall back quickly into training mode without having to reengage the dog or build up a level of energy or excitement.

Secondary and Intermediate Reinforcers

Psychologists tell us that there are only two kinds of reinforcers — primary and secondary. **Secondary reinforcers** (also called **conditioned** reinforcers) are stimuli that animals learn to find reinforcing because they have been paired with primary ones. Although these stimuli are neutral (i.e., they have no naturally appealing or displeasing meaning to the dog), they become reinforcing through association with other stimuli that are reinforcing.

Another type of reinforcer I refer to as **intermediate**, although behavior scientists would disagree with this terminology. I believe that human interaction should be placed somewhere between primary and secondary reinforcement. Initially, the touch of a human hand, the sound of a human voice, has no innate meaning to a dog unless accompanied by pleasure or

Victoria A. Dale

Fig. 2.9. The game of two hoses. I throw one hose, and when Bear returns with it, I give her the other.

pain, whether gentle stroking or loud, frightening shouts. Likewise, puppies must initially be taught to trust human beings and to feel affection for them. So while human contact can become reinforcing independent of primary reinforcers like food, initially it is taught to be reinforcing by association with primary reinforcers. Intermediate reinforcers are not initially reinforcing but become so through association.

Most people believe that dogs are naturally attracted to humans, but this has been proved untrue. Years ago, Clarence Pfaffenberger conducted studies with puppies that were raised without human contact. He found that, unless pups were socialized to humans within the first twelve weeks of life, they never trusted people nor bonded with them. Conscientious breeders are careful to socialize their puppies so that by the time the pups go to their new homes they are so trusting of human beings that the transition is not difficult.

When I have a new litter of pups, I take great care to handle the pups every day, to stroke them, cuddle them, and just hold them. And I talk to them too, even when I know they cannot yet hear me. Later, when they are being weaned, I announce the coming of the food with a lilting, "Puppy, puppy, puppy," and the little ones come running. My puppies never forget me, and years after they have left my home, they still come running to my call.

Not all reinforcement remains conditioned, even though it may have started out that way. A conditioned reinforcer will quickly lose its appeal unless it continues to be associated, at least occasionally, with a primary reinforcer. Yet human interaction doesn't seem to need this. At some stage, human contact alone becomes reinforcing to our dogs, even though in the beginning that contact had to be associated with a primary reinforcer. Our dogs enjoy being with us even when we don't feed or pet them all the time. Sheer proximity to humans is something well-socialized dogs seek out and are willing to work to obtain. Indeed, many dogs remain devoted to their owners even when the owners are abusive to their canine companions.

The lesson to be learned is that a good trainer can create, maintain, and capitalize upon the canine-human bond as long as the pup has had minimal socialization. And once that tie has been created and strengthened, it need not be continuously associated with cookies or other kinds of external reinforcements. In fact, if such a bond has been formed, offering food and toys to the dog can weaken rather than strengthen such a bond because the treats may shift the dog's source of satisfaction away from the trainer.

Other things that are initially reinforcing because of association can also come to be reinforcing in themselves. For example, many dogs do not know how to play with their owners, but come to enjoy it if the trainer takes the time to teach the dog to engage in play activities. I have seen many dogs that showed no natural inclination to chase or carry objects become avid retrievers after force was applied and they found out how fun the game was. For these dogs, the retrieve was at first negatively reinforced by force and positively reinforced by praise or cookies. But once the dogs learned the game, they no longer required reinforcement — the opportunity to retrieve again was all they needed.

Therefore, keep in mind that some reinforcers that initially have to be taught by associating them with others lose the need for such association once the dog has learned to appreciate them. Thus, these intermediate reinforcers may be secondary reinforcers that have become primary.

Unlike primary reinforcers, secondary ones do not come naturally to our dogs. We must teach the dog a secondary or conditioned reinforcer by associating a previously neutral stimulus with an appetitive or aversive one. Normally, these are sounds or visual stimuli that dogs associate with the onset of a pleasurable or painful experience. The words, "Good dog," have no linguistic meaning for the dog until he associates them with something pleasurable like a cuddle, a stroke, or a piece of food. If you have ever squirted your dog with lemon juice to get him to stop barking, you know that the mere presence of the squirt bottle can quiet even the most excited dog.

Secondary reinforcers are generally easier to apply and to bring with us than primary ones. "Good dog" does not spoil if we leave it out in the sun, and even in obedience competition we are allowed to talk to our dog between exercises. In addition, secondary reinforcers are not as dependent upon a dog's internal state. Thus, while a satiated dog may not be reinforced strongly by food, he still may be willing to work for the praise he originally was taught to associate with food.

Amber and the Bank — A Conditioned Reinforcer

When Amber was young I used to take her in the car with me while I ran errands. The teller at the drive-through window of our local bank kept a box of dog biscuits at her window for clients' dogs. I asked her to make Amber earn her biscuit, so each time we arrived the teller would slide the chute out with the biscuit in it and tell Amber to talk. When Amber barked, I would take the biscuit from the chute and give it to her. Amber was a very quick study and soon there was no need for the verbal cue. I would pull in, Amber would bark and out would come the sliding chute with the biscuit. This had continued for a year when the teller was replaced with another who was not friendly to dogs. Yet Amber never stopped barking at that particular drive-through bank, even though she never got another biscuit. In fact, she barked at all drive-through windows for the rest of her life. The sound of the chute, so long associated with the biscuit, had become a conditioned reinforcer. And it remained so for Amber's entire life even though it had long been disassociated from the biscuit that originally gave it meaning and strength.

Clickers

In the world of animal training, a popular and well-known conditioned reinforcer is the clicker, or more appropriately, the sound the clicker makes.

Indeed, a whole school of animal training has grown up around what has come to be called 'clicker training.' There are even several journals and an electronic mail subscription list with large numbers of subscribers. All this from the innocuous sound made by a small plastic box!

There are some definite advantages to clickers that make them popular. First, the sound they make is neutral and therefore, unlike the human voice, does not convey mixed messages to the dog. The trainer who says, in exasperation, "GOOD BOY!" after a dog has finally learned what should have been a simple lesson, may be confusing the dog more than reinforcing him. For although the words themselves may be intended to be reinforcing, the frustration of the trainer cannot be masked, and the emotional overtones that accompany the words may cancel out their intended meaning. While the trainer intends to communicate, "Good," she actually communicates, "Finally, you chowderhead!" Now the dog has conflicting input and, in all probability, will not be reinforced at all. Additionally, clickers make timing easier for people who are not able to deliver a verbal reinforcer at the instant it will have maximum effect (Fig. 2.10). Although I personally prefer to use my voice as a reinforcer to leave my hands free when training, if the use of a clicker makes your training easier and more comprehensible and motivates you to train harder and smarter, by all means use one.

Fig. 2.10. Clickers make a neutral sound that does not convey mixed messages to the dog. The discrete sound of a clicker can improve the timing of your reinforcement.

Remember that anything can function as a conditioned reinforcer if you teach the dog to associate it strongly enough with a primary reinforcer. In fact, natural events often become conditioned reinforcers. These may be sounds or visual or tactile stimuli, and they may be intentionally created or coincidentally formed. My dog, Lark, loved to stare at the beam of light on the floor created by a flashlight. She could hold a fixed position for hours on end watching that beam. She quickly associated the light with the flashlight itself, and eventually the mere presence of a flashlight would cause her to become fixated even in the absence of a beam. Although this had no formal training relevance, when I suffered back pain, Lark was invaluable because she willingly retrieved items from the floor for me. I always thought she liked doing this because the items reminded her of her beloved flashlights.

Although all conditioned reinforcers are initially meaningless to the dog, if paired often enough with a primary reinforcer, they can be used to reinforce the same kinds of behaviors the primary ones do. Remember that conditioned reinforcers can be negative or positive. Dogs that have been boundary trained using underground electronic fences soon learn to jump back from the boundary with as much speed at the sound of the collar's warning tone as they do at the shock itself. They have learned to associate the tone with the shock, and they will act to avoid both.

Bear and the Bed

One night several years ago, I was sitting on my bed watching television. Bear was lying on the bed beside me, Coe and Mikey were lying beside it, and Lark was under it. The television program was not very absorbing, and I soon became fascinated by what Bear was doing. Dominant to the end, she had assumed the role of queen of the hill, and whenever Kate tried to walk by the bed, moving between one napping place under the laundry room sink and the other, the bathtub (Border Collies are very weird), Bear would leap from the bed and drive little Kate back to the laundry room. Poor Kate! She wanted her bathtub bed, but every time she began her journey she was dive-bombed by Bear, the kamikaze Border Collie.

I decided, as leader of the pack, to put an end to Bear's harassment and waited for Kate's next appearance. As soon as her nose appeared around the corner of the door, Bear tensed to jump. I caught her just as she launched herself and pulled her back onto the bed. "No!" I said sternly. "Leave her alone." Bear growled — AT ME! So I shook my finger at her, and she growled again. I could not permit this challenge, so I took Bear by the collar and forced her over on her back (a position of submission). Lark, always the diplomat, left the room. But Coe and Mikey, sensing what promised to be a new version of Saturday night fights, raced over to the bed and began barking hysterically. Just when I had Bear upside down, Kate sensed her opportunity and leapt onto the bed and attacked Bear (Fig. 2.11). There I was, sitting on the bed holding one dog down and pushing another away. Two other dogs were bouncing and barking on the floor. Then the bed broke!

Coe and Mikey took off for parts unknown. Kate leapt off the bed and beat a hasty retreat to her bathtub. Bear and I and the bed hit the floor together. After we all calmed down and I put the bed back together, I noticed a strange phenomenon. Not only was Bear much more respectful of my authority, she approached the bed with great care. To this day, if I am in the bedroom and Bear is misbehaving, all I need do is to point to the bed and say, "Do you want to get up here with me?" and Bear abandons her aggression. Interestingly, she will sleep on the bed with me and she shows no reluctance to get up there on her own. But when I warn her about a behavior that I don't like by using the presence of the bed to remind her of an aversive stimulus, there is no necessity to apply physical force to correct her. My reference to the bed reinforces her non-aggressive behavior — she is more likely to behave with civility to her canine housemates. I don't need to flip her upside down — the bed, my serendipitous conditioned reinforcer, does just fine.

Association and Reinforcement

A conditioned reinforcer works in two ways. First, because it has become associated with a primary reinforcer, it is reinforcing by virtue of that association. It becomes a source of pleasure or discomfort to the dog. If a strong enough connection is formed between the primary and the secondary reinforcers, the dog will work as hard to obtain (or avoid) the conditioned reinforcer as he will for the primary one. For conditioned reinforcers to maintain their strength, they must continue to be paired with primary reinforcers at least occasionally. How often they need to be paired is dependent to some extent upon the intensity of the aversive or appetitive stimulus.

For example, Coe is terrified of the sound of firecrackers. He quickly learned that a whistling sound precedes the firecracker's explosion. Even

53

Fig. 2.11. A conditioned reinforcer — Bear and the bed. **a.** I am watching television with Bear on the bed. **b.** Bear jumps up to prevent Kate from getting to the bathtub. **c.** When I grab Bear and tell her to stop that, Coe and Mikey start to bark and Kate jumps up on the bed to get revenge on Bear. **d.** Then the bed breaks, making a permanent impact on Bear.

though he rarely hears fireworks, any sound that remotely resembles the whistle that precedes the firecracker's bang sends him running for his crate. Although he only hears that whistling sound once a year, those occasional associations are enough to make him try just as hard to avoid the whistle as he would to avoid the firecracker itself.

The second way that conditioned reinforcers work is by providing information about the availability of primary reinforcers (even when the information signals that the primary reinforcement is not available). A number of experiments have proven that animals assign some positive value to information content itself, independent of associations. In one such experiment, pigeons chose to peck keys that gave information about when the primary reinforcer would be available, even though pecking that key did not result in reinforcement. Such preferences are called **observing responses**.

> "There are many demonstrations in the literature that animals will make observing responses, the sole consequence of which is to provide information. This has led to the view that it is just this informativeness that gives conditioned reinforcers their reinforcing power."[1]

Think of all the things you do during the day just to get information. One of the best examples I have heard comes from a friend who talks about the number of times a day she looks at her watch or at a clock. Even if she has no pressing engagement, it is somehow important for her to know what time it is. Another example comes from my own experience. When I travel, I like to have a map open on the seat beside me. For some reason, I find it reinforcing to know just where on the map I am, even if I am hours from my destination and whatever reinforcement I expect to obtain upon arriving. Simply knowing my location is as valuable to me as knowing the time is to my friend.

Creating a Conditioned Reinforcer

Here's how you can create a conditioned positive reinforcer for your dog. Choose some sound or movement that you will use to communicate to your dog that his behavior is correct, that he is doing exactly what you want him to do. Remember that the sound should be neutral. It should have no previous associations for the dog, so avoid words that sound like his name or a command. If you wish to use something other than a word, try to choose a

---

[1] B. Schwartz, S. Robbins. *Learning and Operant Behavior*, W.W. Norton & Co., 1995, pp. 26 - 27

sound that's clear and easy to administer. (Bear's bed is not the ideal conditioned reinforcer to use unless all training is done in the bedroom.)

You may use a clicker if you wish, but bear in mind that if you do, you will not have both hands free to show the dog what you want him to do. Remember also that, because you cannot take the clicker into the competition ring with you, the dog must eventually be weaned from the clicker to another conditioned reinforcer.

As an example of a conditioned reinforcer, let's use the word 'great' uttered with enthusiasm. Initially, that word may not mean much to your dog, although your tone may elicit some tail wagging. You will need to teach the dog that the word 'great' means two separate things. First, it must identify the exact behavior you desire (thus, timing is critical). Second, it must predict that reinforcement is on the way.

Before 'great' can function as a conditioned reinforcer, you must associate it with a primary reinforcer (Fig. 2.12). Take your dog and a bowl of treats to a distraction-free area. Say, "Great!" and give your dog a treat. Do this repeatedly for about five minutes. If your dog gets bored or appears uninterested in the food before the time is up, just put him and the food away. But as long as you have his continuing interest, keep saying the magic word and following it with a treat. Remember, you are not asking the dog for any specific behavior. He need do nothing to earn the treat, and you should not correct him if he nuzzles your hand or tries to get at the food bowl. All you are doing is forming a pleasurable association in his mind between the word 'great' and super goodies, so don't confuse him by introducing commands or negatives like the word 'no' if he pursues the treats a bit too eagerly.

Soon you should recognize a startle response when you say the word 'great.' When the word is uttered, the dog should flick his ears or look at you or, if he is across the room, run over to you. Normally after just a few repetitions, your dog will respond immediately to the word and run to you to get the goodie. If he does this, he is telling you he has begun to understand that the word 'great' means goodies are coming. But this initial reaction does not mean that he recognizes 'great' as being reinforcing in and of itself, so do not stop feeding when you say the word. You must devote considerable time and treats to form a strong conditioned reinforcer (unless you can arrange for something

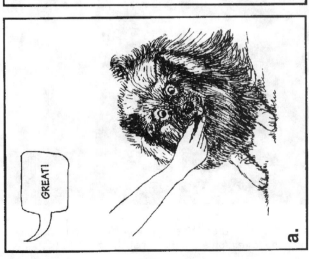

Fig. 2.12. Making the word 'great' into a conditioned reinforcer. **a.** First say, "Great!" and give a treat. **b.** Repeat until the dog gives a startle response when you say the word. **c.** Eventually the word great will make the dog think of getting treats.

as memorable as a falling bed). Once the association has been formed, you will still need to go back and occasionally pair the word with the food to maintain its strength.

So far, all you have done is form the association. Now you need to put the secondary reinforcer in the training context. Tell your dog to sit, assuming that he understands that command, and when he sits, instead of giving him a treat, say, "Great," and then give him the treat (Fig. 2.13). Once you have established the reinforcer this way, increase the length of time between the conditioned reinforcer and the treat. Then ask for more than one repetition of the behavior before giving the treat. The next chapter provides more details on randomizing your reinforcer.

Do not use your conditioned reinforcer without pairing it at least sometimes with a primary reinforcer, or it will quickly lose both its associative and its informative content. That's why it's a good idea to make your conditioned reinforcer a word or sound that you do not use in your everyday

Fig. 2.13. Once the word 'great' has been established as a conditioner reinforcer (left), it can be used to reinforce a behavior such as the sit (right).

interactions with your dog. If you tell your dog he's a good boy a hundred times a day and don't associate those words with a primary reinforcer, the words will not be very effective as a conditioned reinforcer. Their constant use without a primary reinforcer will weaken their meaning. This is one of the reasons why some people find the clicker so convenient. It is unlikely that they would use the clicker outside of the training arena, so they are able to keep the meaning of the click pure.

Praise — What It Is, How It Works

There is much debate about whether praise is a primary or a conditioned stimulus. Perhaps it is a form of the intermediate kind of reinforcement referred to earlier. Clearly most dogs enjoy being sweet talked; just watch a puppy wag his tail and try to kiss your face when you tell him how wonderful he is! Conscientious breeders give the future performance dog a leg up by teaching them, while they are still in the whelping box, that soothing words are accompanied by pleasurable physical sensations. Puppies raised in that atmosphere come to associate human words, touch, and presence with comfort, reassurance, and security. They need not be given food for the human voice and presence to be pleasurable.

So far, we have demonstrated that praise and the presence of a person is an appetitive stimulus. However, it doesn't necessarily follow that because a dog finds something pleasurable, he will be willing to work to obtain it. Some people believe that a dog ought to be willing to work for love. They believe that because they have given the dog food, shelter, and affection, the dog is obligated to reciprocate by offering obedient behavior. "If you really loved me, Buster," they say, "you will not lie down on this *Long Sit* exercise."

But dogs do not understand the concept of moral obligation. They offer us unconditional love and seem to expect the same from us. Although there are dogs that offer stunning performances for little more than a pat on the head and a little praise, most dogs accept all love and affection gladly, return it joyfully, and *still* lie down on the obedience *Long Sit* exercise (Fig. 2.14). Dogs may find praise pleasant, but few will work very hard to obtain it if it is never accompanied by anything else.

If praise is to be reinforcing, it must be desirable enough for the dog to be willing to offer you a behavior for it. Consider the following scenario: You

59

Fig. 2.14. Dogs do not understand the concept of moral obligation. They will give and accept love gladly, but still lie down on the *Long Sit* exercise.

are sitting watching your favorite TV show and enjoying an after-dinner cup of coffee. Your dog wanders into the room, watches you for awhile, and then comes over and nudges your arm. If you ignore him, he nudges harder. The penalty for continuing to ignore him is that coffee is spilled over you, the chair, and your canine buddy. The next time he gives you a gentle nudge, you respond immediately with a pat and a murmured, "Good boy."

This is an example of a reinforced behavior — the nudging of the arm is reinforced by the praise and pat. In this situation, the dog is willing to work for some attention simply because you have been ignoring him. The fact that you are concentrating on something else makes him willing to do something to gain your attention. But look what eventually happens. Sooner or later, the cuteness of the nudging and the novelty of your new designer line, Coffee Stains By Fido, becomes a bore. So you beat Fido to the punch, or to the nudge, and as soon as you see him sidle up to your chair you put the cup down and forestall the nudge by telling him how wonderful he is not to nudge your arm. The words you use don't matter as much as the tone, but you time them so they occur *before* the nudge instead of after it. Basically, you have told him he is wonderful for doing nothing at all. The lesson the dog learns is that attention need not be earned, and that praise and attention require no effort.

In an attempt to prevent dogs from offering attention-seeking behaviors like this around the house, many of us give praise and attention before the dog tells us he is willing to do something to earn them. And most dogs learn that they need offer no behaviors for such human favors — they get it free. Sure they still love us and crave our companionship, sure they find such stimuli appetitive, but there is no need for them to offer any behaviors to obtain them other than to amble into the room and assume the 'ain't I precious' look. No wonder they look askance at a trainer who expects them to pick up a dumbbell from the middle of a mud puddle, just for being told, "Good boy." It's not that they don't love you, it's that you've already taught them that praise and petting are free!

The key to making your praise effective lies in how you use it with your dog. It is important for the dog to learn that he can earn your special attention by offering you behaviors. A friend of mine makes a practice of keeping a bowl of kibble by her TV chair. From the time her dogs come into the house as puppies, they are rewarded with a piece of the kibble and a hug each time they pick something up from the floor. Each time the exploring pup puts its mouth on something, she offers the treat and says in her most her exuberant voice, "Oh, look what you've found!" Soon the pups are picking up anything they can find on the floor and racing to her chair. It's not the kibble that's important as much as the dog's ability to earn the pleased words and attention of the owner. Her puppies get plenty of unconditional love and snuggles on the side, but this kind of game teaches the dog that he can earn special treats, affection, and attention from his owner.

Another friend has trained herself not to use the words, "Good girl," "Good boy," or, "What a good dog you are," in her non-training doggie talk. Instead she uses "Love, Doggie," "What a Love you are," for expressions of general affection. She uses the word 'good' only when it is paired with extra special treats and is used as a deliberate reinforcer for a specific behavior. Thus, she maintains the association of the word 'good' with food and her own special attention, and uses that praise word to reinforce specific behaviors.

Home Schooling

So many of our early contacts with our puppies and our daily encounters with adult dogs contain valuable messages that spill over into the performance part of our dogs' lives. And often we are unaware that what we teach our dogs outside the training building can conflict with and undermine what we are trying to teach in a more formal context. The positive side of this coin is that we can also build valuable foundations for performance training during the non-training time we spend with our dogs. If we understand the role of reinforcement in canine learning and pay attention to our use of reinforcers, we make learning a lifelong game for the dog. Learning becomes something that is not stressful, but something the dog enjoys, something that helps him control his own life.

Training is a game that you will play with your dog as long as he lives. The principles of operant conditioning form the basis of many of the rules of the training game. Dogs that are expected to play by these rules only in formal training and expected to play by other rules (or no rules at all) in other contexts, may come to view training as an unwelcome intrusion. They may be understandably confused by having two sets of rules — those that apply at home, and those that apply to training. It is far better to make your home rules consistent with your training rules. It is far easier for a dog to understand one set of rules than to try to figure out which rules apply in which situation.

Chapter 3. Details, Details, Details

Chapter 2 provided a definition and examples of the most important concept of operant conditioning — reinforcement. If you understand what reinforcement is and how it works, you will be able to design training techniques that work well for you and your dog. You need only one set of rules for both performance training and home obedience. This chapter demonstrates how best to apply the reinforcements you've chosen.

The Principle:
THE WHAT, WHEN AND HOW OF REINFORCEMENT

It's almost as important to understand *what* behaviors you ought to reinforce, *when* and *how* often to reinforce them, and *what* kinds of appetitive stimuli work best, as it is to understand the concept of reinforcement itself. How well reinforcement works is determined by how it is applied.

WHAT Behaviors To Reinforce

Before each training session, you should decide exactly what your expectations are. If you plan to use reinforcement at all, it is essential that you decide which specific behaviors you will reinforce before they happen. Do you want the dog to offer the entire behavior before you reinforce, or are you willing instead to reinforce just a part of that behavior? Will you withhold reinforcement until the dog offers you a perfect performance, or will you reinforce his first attempt?

The answers to these questions depend to a great degree on the kind of behaviors you want to teach and the level at which the dog is working. Complex behaviors need to be reinforced one piece at a time — the more difficult the behavior, the more necessary is frequent reinforcement. Otherwise, it's easy for the learning dog to become discouraged and give up. If you wanted your daughter to improve her grades in school from C's to A's, you would not wait to reinforce her until she brought home A's, but would respond positively each time her grades showed even the slightest improvement. It's important for both people and dogs that slight progress toward complex or difficult goals be recognized and rewarded.

Shaping a Behavior

The technique of reinforcing behaviors as they gradually approach a final goal is called *shaping a behavior by successive approximations*. It is one of the most positive and motivating strategies a trainer can use because it encourages the dog to keep trying, even if he has not yet attained the finished behavior.

One of the most striking applications of shaping is teaching a dog to retrieve. In the past, many obedience beginners dropped out after completing the Novice level because they were reluctant to teach the retrieve. This reluctance was partly due to the way the retrieve was taught. Dog and owner were almost always introduced to the dumbbell in a negative way. The owner was told to pry the often resistant dog's mouth open and insert the dumbbell. She was then instructed to hold the dumbbell in the dog's mouth despite the struggles of the dog to spit it out. The use of so much force so early in the training routine often resulted in a dog who was afraid of the dumbbell and a trainer who was disillusioned with the whole process of obedience training and thought, "If that's what I have to do to him to get him to retrieve, it isn't worth it!"

With shaping by successive approximations, the retrieve can be introduced and taught in a much more positive way. The process begins with the trainer reinforcing any attention the dog pays to the dumbbell at all and continues as the trainer reinforces each incremental step the dog takes toward the dumbbell. No physical pressure is applied.

For example, you might sit with a bowl of food at your side and the dumbbell in your hand. The first time the dog even looks at the dumbbell, you would use your conditioned reinforcer such as a clicker or the word 'good,' and then give him a piece of tasty food. You may have to wave the dumbbell in front of him at first, if he doesn't want to look at it. If your dog is motivated by food, it won't take him long to form a pleasant association with the sight of the dumbbell. Once the dog is consistently paying attention to the dumbbell instead of the food bowl or your hand with the food in it, raise the criteria. You might withhold reinforcement until the dog takes a step toward the dumbbell, then until he put his nose on the dumbbell. Eventually, you would withhold the treat until the dog puts his mouth on the dumbbell (Fig. 3.1), then until the dumbbell is in his mouth. You might have to rub a bit of food on the dumbbell to get the dog to initially open his mouth over the dumbbell. Once the dog is reaching for and grabbing the dumbbell, you would ask for behaviors that are more and more like the finished retrieve.

This shaping by successive approximations not only makes the initial exposure to the dumbbell more pleasant for both the handler and the dog, it encourages the dog to engage in the behavior voluntarily. Because the dog is not physically forced to take the dumbbell, it is easier for him to learn what a retrieve is. Learning processes that are devoid of fear and compulsion work well with most dogs. Trainers need to be generous with reinforcement, especially during the introduction to an exercise. Once dogs learn to play the shaping game, they will eagerly offer a multitude of behaviors from which the trainer can choose. But if they are not reinforced enough, they may give up on the game before they really learn the rules.

Fig. 3.1. Shaping the retrieve. At this stage, the trainer witholds the treat until the dog puts his mouth on the dumbbell.

Painting By Numbers: The Anatomy of an Exercise

Before you pick up the collar and leash to start training an exercise, you should have a mental picture of how the final exercise should look. You then break the exercise down into all of its components and that is how you will teach it — one part at a time. For example, the final obedience retrieve includes the dog leaving your side on command, running directly to the dumbbell, picking it up without fumbling it, and then returning briskly with the dumbbell held firmly in his mouth. You should teach and reinforce each part of the exercise separately. In addition, you do not necessarily need to teach the components of the retrieve exercise in the order in which the finished behavior will occur. The order in which you teach each of the steps in the chain of behaviors is not as important as is the attention given to reinforcing each successive step in the series.

Timing: The Training Keystone

It is not necessary to get the food to the dog immediately after he offers the correct behavior. Indeed, if you are shaping a retrieve, the dumbbell is in the dog's mouth anyway. However, you must give your conditioned reinforcer at exactly the right moment. The dog needs to be given the information that his behavior is correct *immediately* after he performs it, not after you pause to decide whether he did it well enough for you to reinforce him. If you've timed your conditioned reinforcer well, the timing with which you deliver the food is not as crucial.

Before you begin training each exercise, it is essential that you decide how much of a progression toward the desired behavior you will require before giving the reinforcer. In early training, when you are introducing your dog to an exercise or to a new training device like a jump, a dumbbell or a metal scent discrimination article, you should reward each correct behavior. In those early stages, you are not only reinforcing a behavior, you are forming a positive association with the unfamiliar object and, more generally, with the introduction of new things.

Although it's hard to reinforce too much during the learning stages, careful analysis and appropriate timing are the keys to communicating which behaviors are desirable. Pay strict attention to everything your dog does. Plan ahead so that you can pay exclusive attention to each small piece of behavior your dog offers. Lack of attention and inappropriate timing can easily confuse and frustrate your dog. Reinforcement should be given in a way that keeps the dog offering a little more with each action. It should be frequent enough to keep him working, but not so frequent that he continues to be reinforced for offering the same behaviors over and over. Like most intelligent students, our dogs will offer the lowest minimal behavior that is met with reinforcement. Therefore, inducing additional effort not only moves you closer to your goals, it teaches the dog that trying will be rewarded.

Cueing the Behavior

Chapter 1 introduced the four steps of training: creating a behavior, defining it, cueing it, and maintaining it. Now that you have created and defined the behavior, it is time to cue it. The dog must be taught to associate the behavior with a specific command. In addition, he must learn that the behavior will be reinforced only after the command is given. That does not mean that our dogs are not allowed to offer behaviors associated with obedience exercises at other times. Obviously our dogs will sit and lie down independent of command, but those behaviors will not be reinforced.

You should wait to assign a cue word to the behavior until the animal is offering something close to the ideal behavior. Let's say you want to teach your dog to lie down, then roll over onto one hip and tuck a front paw under. Many trainers prefer this position for the *Long Down* exercises in Novice and Open obedience. You plan to teach this position by shaping it and reinforcing successive approximations. You might initially reinforce the dog just for lowering his head, then for stretching his forelegs forward, then for touching his elbows to the ground, for rolling on to one hip, and finally for tucking the front paw. If you were to say, "Down" for each small increment of behavior, the meaning of the word 'down' would be constantly changing (Fig. 3.2). It is unrealistic for a trainer to expect her dog to be able to abstract the common or progressive elements for these different behaviors and synthesize them so he can ultimately say, "Ah, that's what that command means." Far better to delay the cue word until the dog has offered a behavior that closely resembles what you want.

There is no need to introduce vocabulary to your dog's performances at the beginning of the training process. Dogs assign meaning to words by associating them with particular contexts, just as you may understand the meaning of a word best when it is used in a sentence. In fact, words mean far less to the dog than does the context in which the behavior occurs. A cue uttered in the presence of a correct behavior and in conjunction with a

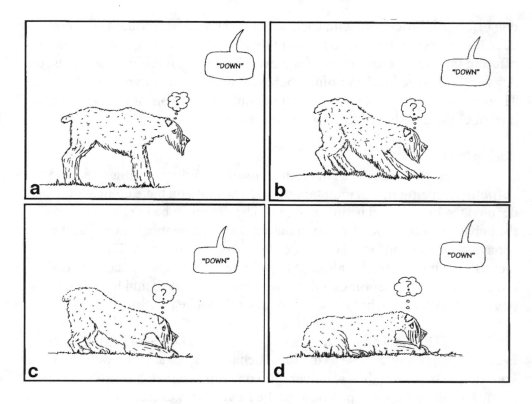

Fig. 3.2. It is advisable not to assign a word to the behavior until the animal is offering something close to the ideal behavior. This dog doesn't know which of his movements is the correct response to the command.

conditioned reinforcer (i.e., "Good down," and a treat) provides far more information to the dog than a continuous "Down, down, down" chant as the dog gradually lowers himself to the ground.

It is especially important to hold off introducing the cue word for complex behaviors — those that involve a series of separate actions. Let's use the example of the retrieve again. The command, "Take it," actually asks the dog to offer a number of different behaviors. He must leave the handler's side, run to the dumbbell, pick it up, bring it directly back to the trainer and then sit in front of her to deliver it. Although some links in this chain have their own corresponding commands (the return from the retrieve is associated with the word 'come' and the sit in front is often indicated by the command, 'front'), there are still many parts to the retrieve itself. It is best not to put a retrieve on cue until the dog is reaching for the dumbbell and grasping it firmly in his mouth. The command therefore comes relatively late in the learning sequence. If the retrieve is trained using shaping by successive approximation, most dogs reach for the dumbbell willingly at the mere sight of it. There is no need for a command at this stage of training.

WHEN To Reinforce

The delivery of reinforcement depends on more than just the dog performing a certain behavior. What if you are practicing the obedience *Recall* exercise and, when your dog is halfway back to you, a car backfires loudly? The dog pauses momentarily, looks toward the sound, and then continues in. Do you want to reinforce that recall at all? If so, how? Clearly it is not a recall that you wish to take into the ring — you want your dog to come straight in to you regardless of distractions. At the same time, the dog has shown evidence of thinking through a rather difficult problem. If this is the dog's first exposure to such a situation, you may want to reinforce him for overcoming the distraction. Therefore, you would praise lavishly: "Great job!" If your dog had been exposed to a variety of different environments and noises, you might want to be more mild in your reinforcement: "Nice work, but let's try a little harder next time." And if you are working with a seasoned dog, you might want to withhold reinforcement entirely: "C'mon Buster, let's try that again."

Schedules of Reinforcement

Few performance events allow the handler to reinforce the dog during an exercise. And no performance event allows food or toys or the games associated with them in the competition ring. The dog must learn to offer an entire performance routine without the reinforcements most frequently offered in training. The trainer must acclimate the dog to offer an entire set of behaviors with only reinforcements that can legally be given in the ring — usually praise and gentle petting between exercises. Thus, before being entered in competition, the dog must be taught to perform without food, toys, or games for finite periods of time. The best way to do this is to design an appropriate schedule of reinforcement.

There is no one perfect reinforcer and reinforcement schedule. The type of reinforcement should vary according to the temperaments of both dog and trainer, the task, the environment, and the relationship between the trainer and dog. In the laboratory, some of these variables are insignificant or under the control of the experimenter, and scientists rarely have close relationships with experimental animals. In addition, the laboratory environment can be totally controlled. In contrast, the dog trainer has to pay attention to each and every factor that might impact the dog's work.

Although there is no perfect schedule of reinforcement, there are schedules that are effective with some exercises and not with others. This chapter outlines four different schedules, describes the circumstances in which each works best, and tells how to know when to change the schedule. Note that certain behaviors are more amenable to some schedules than to others.

Rule of Thumb

Boring, repetitive behaviors normally last longer on a variable schedule while those that require decisions or extra effort on the part of the dog may require a more constant reinforcement schedule.

You need to know your dog, your own limitations, and the degree of difficulty of the behaviors your dog will be required to perform. You should also have some idea of how the environment will affect your dog's learning. Before beginning a training session, therefore, it is essential to decide which schedules of reinforcement you will use for each of the components of the exercises you plan to work on.

In general, when a dog is first learning a behavior, you should reinforce every correct performance of that behavior. This is called a **continuous reinforcement schedule**. You will also want to use a continuous reinforcement schedule when you begin to proof a dog by exposing him to new sites or distractions, such as having a little kid eat an ice cream cone in front of him. In addition, many trainers think that exercises where the dog is responsible for making the correct decision, such as the *Scent Discrimination* exercise, should be continuously reinforced.

Just as there is no single correct reinforcer that is appropriate for all occasions, there is no single schedule of reinforcement that a trainer can apply all of the time. For example, you may have moved your dog from a continuous schedule to less frequent reinforcements. But if you go to a different location and your dog seems to have forgotten the behavior, you may need to back up and reinforce more often. You may temporarily need to reinforce on a continuous schedule. When your dog's performance tells you that a particular environment is no longer a distraction, reinforcement may be given less often.

Remember that the ultimate goal is the performance ring and that food and toys are not permitted there. Once the dog is offering a behavior on cue reliably, you should quickly reduce the frequency of reinforcement. By keeping a dog on one schedule of reinforcement, especially on a fixed schedule, for too long a time, you may cause the dog to view the schedule itself as an important environmental cue. When the food cue is removed, the dog may be unable to perform the behavior.

The Four Schedules of Reinforcement

Behaviorists have defined four different schedules of reinforcement. Although the differences are really in degree rather than in kind, it is important for the trainer to have all of these schedules in her training bag.

Fixed Ratio: In a fixed ratio schedule of reinforcement, the reinforcer is given after a specific and unchanging *number* of correct behaviors. You might, for example, reward after every five steps of correct heeling or after every leg of a heeling pattern. 'Fixed' means that the number does not change. 'Ratio' means that you are looking for a specific number of correct behaviors — good fronts, jumps, etc. A continuous reinforcement schedule, therefore, has a fixed ratio of one.

Fixed Interval: In fixed interval reinforcement, instead of reinforcing for a specific number of correct behaviors, the dog is reinforced after maintaining a behavior for a specific period of *time*. For example, you might reinforce after every two minutes of a correctly held sit-stay. If you choose to use this schedule, you will have to be careful. Dogs have a very good sense of timing and will come to expect the reinforcement after whatever fixed interval has been adopted by the trainer. For example, dogs that have been extensively campaigned in the Open obedience class quickly learn the intervals involved in the three minute *Long Sit* and five minute *Long Down* exercises. If a judge loses track of time or the handlers take an excessively long time to return, many dogs begin to fidget or even change position as the stays go beyond the ingrained intervals.

Since humans are creatures of habit, we tend to use ring criteria in practice sessions, limiting ourselves to exactly those exercises required in competition (such as Novice level stays of one and three minutes). But dogs are highly sensitive to environmental circumstances, and they soon learn to maintain the requested behavior for only the interval that the trainer

71

reinforces. If the interval of reinforcement is fixed, it may ultimately control the duration of the behavior the dog is willing to offer. Many trainers, therefore, condition their dogs to a much longer fixed interval than will be necessary for ring performance, reasoning that if the dog is taught to expect the trainer to return after ten minutes, he will not expect an earlier return and thus will not break his position in anticipation. They hope that a dog who is comfortable doing a 10-minute sit will think a mere 3-minute one is easy. While this works for inexperienced dogs, those that are shown extensively will learn to take their cues from the environment and use the ring itself to predict the intervals at which their handler returns, releases, and reinforces them.

Variable Ratio: On this schedule the dog is reinforced after a variable number of correct behaviors. For example, as your dog learns to heel better and better, you might begin to withhold reinforcement for longer distances of correct heeling. But you should vary the number of steps after which you reinforce. Don't wait for the whole pattern to be over before reinforcing. Instead, reinforce at different and unpredictable points in the pattern — perhaps after the first leg, then the third step of the second leg, and then after the tenth step of the last leg. Your objective is to make your reinforcements so unpredictable that the dog will continue to work because he always expects that the next correct step will earn him the cookie (Fig. 3.3).

Variable Interval: When using this schedule of reinforcement, you vary the amount of time between reinforcements. One time you might reinforce after 10 seconds, then after a minute, then 15 seconds, then 45 seconds. By varying the intervals of your reinforcements, you prevent the dog from defining his behavior in terms of any specific interval. Although the dog knows he will be reinforced, he is just never sure when. This schedule works better than either of the fixed ones because it makes it difficult for the dog to anticipate reinforcement. As long as the dog thinks there is a chance that the reinforcement still may come, he is likely to continue to offer the behavior over a longer period of time.

> ### Note:
> Behaviors put on variable schedules of reinforcement are more resistant to extinction than are those on other schedules.

It's important to put your dog on a variable schedule of reinforcement as early in your training program as you can. Your goal is to obtain an entire ring performance without any primary reinforcement. The reason for this should be clear. Dogs that are constantly reinforced in training, then taken into the show ring and given no reinforcement, become confused and demotivated very quickly. These dogs have learned to use the constant reinforcement in training as a source of information and reassurance that they are doing things right. When you suddenly stop reinforcing, the sudden lack of information worries and confuses your dog, who then loses confidence in himself and in you.

Dogs that are introduced to variable schedules of reinforcement in training sessions become used to working for longer periods of time and through many different behaviors with little or no reinforcement. They do not depend on constant reinforcement to reassure them that they are right. Indeed, it is the variable schedule that gives them faith that what they're doing is just fine. These dogs believe there will be reinforcement if they just work a little harder and keep trying a little longer.

Fig. 3.3. A dog on a variable schedule of reinforcement will continue to work in the hope that the next step will produce the treat.

WHAT Reinforcers To Use

Quantity, quality, and variety of reinforcers all affect the dog's performance. Occasional rewards of a dog's special favorite food or toy seem to reenergize the dog, to motivate him to try harder and perform better. If you vary the kind and the amount of reinforcers, your dog will learn more quickly than if you use the same treat and feed the same amount each time. If you come to the training session with several different kinds of food such as chicken, hot dogs, and some plain old kibble, you will enhance the ways in which you can tell your dog, "Well done!" If the dog makes exceptional progress or masters a difficult exercise that day, some leftover steak just might underline the correct behavior and add an exclamation point to a job well done.

Changing from reinforcer to reinforcer, from kibble to steak and from steak to kibble, adds a variety that dogs find most reinforcing. Let your variety be determined by the preferences of your dog and the plenitude of your pantry. Use Cheerios or baby carrots for fat-free treats. It's also a good idea to have several toys available and to switch to them occasionally, just for variety. Remember, reinforcement is relative, and what may be reinforcing at one time may not be at another.

Quantity of Reinforcement

The amount of reinforcement used is particularly significant to performance. Although all trainers aim for a performance that requires no primary reinforcement, careful attention to the amount of food used in training helps a trainer maximize both the speed and enjoyment of the dog's learning process.

Although dogs should be liberally reinforced in the beginning stages of learning, you don't want your dog to expect such generous reinforcement throughout the process. This is the concept of **least possible reinforcement**. Least possible reinforcement is the smallest amount of reinforcement that will maintain the dog's behavior. Good trainers constantly walk a tightrope. They want to give enough reinforcement to keep the dog motivated to try for more, but not so much that the dog is satisfied with what he has already done and content to put only minimal effort (or none at all) into his work.

Jackpots

At the opposite end of the quantity scale is the **jackpot**. The term originated in gambling casinos and describes the payoff a person playing the slot machines hopes to receive (Fig. 3.4). The payoff is large and unpredictable. It is exciting and motivating just because it is so unpredictable. A casino calibrates its machines to payoff frequently enough for the gambler to have a reasonable hope of obtaining a payoff, but not so often that jackpots become routine. Dogs respond to jackpots in much the same way that people do. The jackpot adds a dash of excitement to training, and it motivates most dogs to try harder. Jackpotting is appealing because of both the quantity of reinforcement and its variable nature; it demonstrates the power of varying both quantity and delivery of reinforcement. The hope of a jackpot is enough to keep a person gambling for days. It is also enough to motivate a dog to higher levels of intensity in training.

A jackpot for a dog could be a whole handful of wonderful food (Fig. 3.5), or it could be a rousing game of tug after a particularly good performance, for solving an especially difficult problem, or for mastering a new exercise. The key is that it is unexpected, but not so unexpected that the dog will be discouraged from trying his best to earn it. Although the timing of the jackpot is up to the trainer, a jackpot given at the end of a training session has limited use since the dog will not be asked to offer any other behaviors that

Fig. 3.4. A jackpot is a large and unpredictable payoff. The jackpot motivates the dog to a higher level of achievement.

Fig. 3.5. This dog is being given a container full of cheese as a jackpot.

could be affected by the treat. Jackpotting can also be used to countercondition a dog that has become fearful of the ring (see Chapter 6).

Internal Reinforcers

Some behaviors are **self-reinforcing**. That is, the behavior itself reinforces the animal and no external reward is required. Most of us know dogs who are fanatic retrievers. From puppyhood on, these dogs carry objects whenever possible. Visitors are invariably presented with slimy tennis balls and slippery toys, the dog's way of inviting them to play a good game of fetch. The opportunity to chase and retrieve the ball is so reinforcing to these dogs that they are immune to all sorts of human rejection, including guests' frantic and sometimes angry attempts to push them away. Obviously, such retrievers need not be externally reinforced for retrieving.

One of the long-range goals for your performance dog is that he come to regard the performance of the exercises as reinforcing in themselves. As dogs progress in their training, gain confidence in what is expected of them, and come to see the training and the performance sessions as occasions of enjoyment, many of them become more eager to perform the exercises than to obtain the treats. It is especially helpful if the exercises arouse the dogs' natural instincts (Fig. 3.6). Even dogs that are not natural retrievers may become fanatic retrievers once the exercise has been taught, because the thrown dumbbell incites their prey drive. Many dogs taught heeling or jumping using positive reinforcement come to enjoy bouncing at their handlers' sides or racing over jumps. Let your dog be the guide. If he tells you that the exercises themselves are what are most reinforcing, slacken off on the treats and the toys. It's much easier to work with a dog that loves performing the exercises than with one who is doing it only for reinforcement.

Much of the popularity of agility and flyball are due to the immediately reinforcing nature of the activities. Dogs strain at their leashes, fly around the course, and leap at the opportunity to do it all over again. Once these exercises have been learned, they are so reinforcing that it is difficult to imagine the dogs being willing to take time out during competition to eat tidbits of food, even if it were legal to offer them. No dog is born with an agility instinct, but if the dog is carefully trained, he comes to love the sport for itself. The good trainer manages to couple the dog's love of physical activity with confidence in the various exercises themselves to create the joyful completion of a winning round.

Don't be too quick to separate formal training from play in your training sessions or in the ring. There is no rule against teaching the dog small and subtle games that can be played in the ring between exercises. Good trainers don't just wait for a dog to begin to enjoy an obedience exercise or hope that instinct will kick in. They make a concentrated effort to teach the dog that the exercise itself is fun. They tease the dog and rev him up and show him how to have a wonderful time. For some dogs, this takes a lot of work; trainers may spend more physical effort convincing the dog that they are enjoying themselves than they do actually training a behavior. But it surely pays off in the end.

If you are lucky enough to have a dog who is naturally reinforced by a performance exercise, it is important to remember that self-reinforcing behaviors should not be externally reinforced. Indeed, studies suggest that if behaviors that were originally self-reinforcing are externally reinforced, they lose their self-reinforcing property.

An experiment done with children in primary school who enjoyed reading demonstrated this danger very well. All of the children chosen for the

Victoria A. Dale

Fig. 3.6. Some behaviors are self-reinforcing. This dog needs no external reward for herding sheep.

experiment freely chose to read books in their spare time. Yet after an experimental period in which they were reinforced externally for reading by being given tokens that could be exchanged for candy or video games, the children did not choose to read again in the absence of some sort of external reinforcement. The introduction of external reinforcement diminished the reinforcing nature of the activity itself.

Observe what your dog chooses to do in his own free time. Chances are that he will engage in activities that reinforce him naturally. In addition, pay attention to his reactions to the behaviors you have taught him. If some of those behaviors appear to be reinforcing in and of themselves, do not reinforce them externally. A dog that loves to retrieve does not need a piece of food as a reward for a fast, flashy retrieve naturally offered. All he really needs is the chance to retrieve again. Remember that food offered after this behavior may actually teach the dog to cease to offer such retrieves in the absence of food!

You: The Most Important Reinforcer Of All

Some fellow dog trainers and I visited Marine World and spent most of the day watching the animals, the trainers, and the methods of training. One of the things that captured my attention was the differences in the relationships between the trainers and the animals. The woman who trained the tigers simply threw chunks of meat in front of them when they exhibited the cued behaviors. Although she did occasionally touch the tigers, she exhibited no real affection for them (can't say I blame her; they were a surly bunch). Primary reinforcers so impersonally delivered can have little or no connection with the person who delivers them.

On the other hand, the trainers of the marine mammals and of the birds seemed to relish physical contact with their wards. Although all of the performers were rewarded with food, the whales, dolphins, parrots, owls, and cockatiels were given food directly by their trainers, often with a stroke or affectionate word. Now I realize that no trainer in her right mind would want to put her hand between a tiger and a sirloin steak, but the way that these trainers delivered their reinforcements was radically different. There was demonstrable affection between the whales and their trainers, and there appeared to be a similar relationship between the birds and their people, too.

In fact, one of the most interesting differences became evident when the animals misbehaved. When a tiger said, "Not today" (it was very hot), the trainer uttered a sharp, "No!" and insisted the animal repeat the performance. If one of the birds, on the other hand, suffered an attack of amnesia (and the birds minded the heat as much as the tigers), the trainer made a joke of it and simply gently insisted the bird repeat the performance. The same held true of the marine mammal trainers. Although all trainers insisted the animals perform the behavior correctly (even the baby whale, who was obviously serving an apprenticeship, had to go back several times till he got it right), the tiger trainer was the only one who administered obvious aversives.

As the afternoon wore on and we got progressively more hot and tired, we migrated to the whale and dolphin amphitheater. The shows of the day were over, and the two killer whales were lounging in the outside pool. As the trainers passed by in the course of their non-training duties, the whales swam over to them, and the trainers invariably took time out from their chores to sit down beside them and stroke and talk to them. One trainer, obviously on her way home and dressed in street clothes, stopped, took her high heels off, and sat down beside her charges to give both some good-bye pats. There was an easy affection there that surely enhanced the training relationship. The fact that the trainers themselves seemed to enjoy this camaraderie as much as their charges went a long way in convincing me that there is more to reinforcement than merely food and toys.

The Personal Touch

When one of my dogs does a really good job or solves a particularly difficult problem, it's a genuine pleasure to tell him what a wonderful dog he is and to give him a hug along with the treat. Even my conditioned reinforcer, "Great job!" is scarcely neutral. Any tones, touches, or expressions that reflect the relationship between the dog and trainer should be more reinforcing than ones that are delivered neutrally.

It seems clear that in addition to the nature, timing, and amount of reinforcement, it matters very much *how* the reinforcement is given (Fig. 3.7) and by *whom*! It's one thing to toss a piece of liver on the floor and tell the dog that he is good and yet another to give him the food from your hand. When you deliver the reinforcement personally, the food becomes associated with your physical presence and with the relationship that you and your dog have formed. Verbal reinforcement that you give to your dog means more to him than verbal reinforcement coming from a stranger, no matter how warm and genuine the stranger's reinforcement is! And there is no reason not to

Fig. 3.7. It matters very much how the reinforcement is given, and by whom.

Details, Details, Details

believe that the same holds true of primary reinforcements — that a treat given by you has more positive meaning and is more valuable than a treat given by a stranger. The attention you give your dog in the process of delivering the reinforcement can sometimes be more significant than the treat itself. And that is as it should be! A successful trainer must be regarded by her dog as much more than merely a dispenser of goodies (Fig. 3.8).

You should work to make yourself the strongest primary reinforcer of all. Your dog should be willing to work to obtain your presence and attention. For dogs that are thus reinforced, the offering of food or toys may actually reduce the power of the reinforcement that their relationship holds. I want my dog to focus on me, not the treat, when he wants information, confirmation, and approval. The relationship we continually build with our dogs is the best way to set that process in motion. If your own presence is not reinforcing to your dog and he is indifferent to you, then no food, no matter how good, and no games, no matter how exciting, can fill the void that this emptiness creates.

Fig. 3.8. The successful trainer is regarded by her dog as more than just a dispenser of goodies.

A Reminder

If you understand what reinforcement is and how it works, you hold the key to training your dog. You now have the ability to tell him when he's a little bit right, a lot right, or perfectly right. And you can also tell him that you love him at the same time. The trainer who knows what her dog will work for, how and when to deliver the goodie, and when to change the schedule, the quantity, and the nature of the reinforcements, is a long way ahead of one who merely spits hot dogs for correct fronts. The trainer who takes this knowledge and extends it beyond the training ring to the home situation has created a seamless environment in which the dog need not differentiate the happiness he finds in everyday life from the training situation. For the performance dog, this is the best of all possible worlds.

4. When To Say No

The Principle:
AVERSIVES

The most heated debates among dog trainers center around the use of aversives. Trainers have argued for years about which ones work, what is too harsh, and whether to use aversives at all. The fact that this debate has lasted so long and has resulted in such acrimonious exchanges among otherwise congenial trainers is proof that many people don't understand what aversives are or how they work. Opponents believe that aversives are synonymous with pain and suffering. Because they define aversives in this way, they often characterize trainers who use them as abusive people who do not genuinely care for their dogs. Regardless of how a trainer feels about aversives, it is essential to gain a comprehensive understanding of them, if only because there is so much misunderstanding about what aversives are and how they function.

Many dog trainers are introduced to the benefits of positive reinforcement only after they have trained with methods that involve heavy use of aversives. These trainers have experienced first hand the effects on both dog and handler of training with purely aversive methods. They have seen their dogs become anxious and frightened at the sight of the collar and the leash and perform in a stressed fashion. Because of these negative associations and the guilt they feel about causing their dogs pain, they vow never to do that to a dog again. But the science of operant conditioning doesn't deal only with positive reinforcement. Correctly used aversives can be beneficial. This chapter discusses how aversives work, whether they should be used, and if so, when in the training process it is best to introduce them.

Aversives — A Review

Aversive is the opposite of appetitive. Just as an appetitive stimulus is something your dog finds pleasing, an **aversive** is something he finds unpleasant. Many aversives occur naturally. Sunshine on a hot day is something most dogs find uncomfortable enough that they are willing to take action to avoid it — they seek shade. Mother dogs will growl and push a puppy away if the little one nurses too roughly or bites too hard. Aversive stimuli are as important to wild animals as appetitive since they provide information about what the animal needs to avoid in order to survive.

In a similar way, aversives are quite valuable in dog training. They convey information to the dog, and sometimes knowing what not to do is as important as knowing what to do. Aversives serve two different, albeit related, functions in training. First, they play a role in **negative reinforcement**. Let's refer again to the example of a dog seeking shade on a hot day. The heat of the sun is aversive to the dog — it makes him uncomfortable. So the dog seeks shade, which is really just the absence of sunlight. The shade removes the aversive and so is negatively reinforcing since the dog is more likely to seek shade the next time he is exposed to sunlight. The removal of the aversive plays a role in the reinforcement of shade-seeking behavior, and thus constitutes negative (removal of stimulus) reinforcement (increases the likelihood of the behavior being offered again).

Second, aversives may serve to eliminate a behavior. Look back at the example of a mother dog growling at her pups who are playing too roughly. In this case, aversives in the form of growling and pushing the puppies away are intended to eliminate a behavior — the rough play of the puppies. When an aversive is applied to eliminate a behavior, it is termed **punishment.** There is much confusion between negative reinforcement and punishment. The confusion exists because both concepts involve the application of aversives. This chapter explains both concepts fully.

Punishment

Although both punishment and negative reinforcement involve the application of aversive stimuli, there are profound dissimilarities between the two concepts. The object of punishment is the elimination of a behavior. If I want a dog to stop sniffing during the obedience stay exercises, I might tap him on his nose. This is an application of an aversive stimulus. "You sniff," I tell him, "and this unpleasant thing will happen." If the punishment works and the dog understands why it is being applied, he will avoid further unpleasant taps on the nose by eliminating sniffing from his repertoire of stay behaviors.

Not only does punishment differ from reinforcement in that it seeks to eliminate rather than to reinforce a behavior, it also differs in the timing of its application. Punishment immediately *follows* the unwanted behavior, and there is no behavior that the dog can offer to cancel it. By applying an aversive immediately after an unwanted behavior, the intent is to cause the dog to *avoid* that behavior in the future, not to offer it.

Types of Punishment

Just as there are two kinds of reinforcers, positive and negative, there are also two kinds of punishment: positive and negative. It helps if you apply the mathematical model again. **Positive punishment** is the *addition* of an aversive stimulus following the unwanted action, as in the taps on the nose or the growl and push of the mother dog.

Negative punishment is the *removal* of an appetitive stimulus following an unwanted behavior. Just as you might remove driving privileges from a teenager who gets a speeding ticket, so might you remove a toy from a dog who growls when you approach him while he is playing. In each of these cases, punishment is applied in an attempt to eliminate specific behaviors: speeding and growling. The goal of these punishments is for teenager and dog to avoid these behaviors in the future so that they may keep the things they find appealing — driving privileges and the toy.

Conditioned Punishers

The conditioned punisher is a parallel concept to the conditioned reinforcer. The two concepts are taught in much the same way, by prefacing the application of the appetitive or aversive stimulus with a sound or other stimulus that is initially neutral for the dog. For example, you might use certain words like 'no' or 'ahh, ahh' before an aversive stimulus such as leash pressure or a collar pop. You want the dog to associate the word with the stimulus so that the word itself will eventually serve to suppress the unwanted behavior.

One day when Coe was just a young dog, we were returning to the house after a walk. As we approached the back porch door, I noticed that the cleaning woman had arrived and was working in the kitchen. Before I had a chance to grab Coe's collar, he saw what he thought was a stranger in his house and leapt, feet first, at the glass door. My shout of "No!" more in horror at what could happen to Coe than as an attempt at an obedience command, preceded the crash and shower of broken glass as he hit the door (Fig. 4.1). Although, blessedly, Coe was not hurt (nor did the woman die of a heart attack), the word 'no' assumed enormous significance for him. Not only has he never again leapt at a glass door, he has managed to generalize the word 'no' to other situations, and when he hears it, he immediately stops whatever he is doing and looks at me.

The Shock Collar — A Conditioned Punisher

Conditioned punishers are especially important for those who use aversive devices like shock collars. Although it is the shock and not the collar that the dog finds aversive, the dog comes to associate the presence of the collar around his neck with the application of the shock itself. Dogs use the environment as a reliable predictor of whether aversive or appetitive stimuli are present. Just as a dog quickly learns that he will not be reinforced in some circumstances, such as in the performance ring, he also learns that he may be punished in others, such as when he is wearing the collar.

Dogs learn equally well that the absence of the collar means that the shock is not forthcoming. Once this happens, they are likely to revert to their undesirable behaviors. A good trainer can capitalize on the status of the shock collar as a conditioned reinforcer by having the dog wear a dummy shock collar instead of the real thing. (Most shock collar kits come complete with both real and dummy collars.) The presence of the dummy collar is interpreted by the dog to mean that punishment is possible. The collar itself becomes an informative device necessary to keep the dog obedient to commands, and the trainer need not carry all the other paraphernalia necessary for a shock to actually be administered. Similarly, the word 'no' carries weight for Coe even when we are not on the back porch — it is easily generalized by him.

Fig. 4.1. The word 'no' became a conditioned punisher for Coe when it was fortuitously linked with the breaking glass when he jumped through a door.

Does Punishment Work?

The efficacy of punishment has been debated ever since Thorndyke postulated the term as the opposite of the term 'reward.' Thorndyke himself argued that the two terms were not exactly parallel because the behavior for which the animal was to be punished had to have initially been reinforced by something for it to occur at all. Therefore, the punishment does not occur in a void, but is used to eliminate a behavior that is already being reinforced by something else. Later, B. F. Skinner, the psychologist most commonly associated with the development of operant conditioning, criticized punishment, claiming that it made only a negative contribution to the behaviors of animals because it offered no alternative behavior as a means for the animal to obtain reinforcement.

According to Skinner, punishment contains no constructive advice. It contains no instruction for the animal about appropriate behaviors. Although it may tell the dog what *not* to do, it does not tell him what he *should* do. While this may be fine for behaviors that are two dimensional (e.g., bark or don't bark), it is less informative when there are a variety of alternative behaviors available, some of which are equally unacceptable.

The lack of information is one of the reasons it is difficult to teach a dog to heel by popping his collar when he is out of position. Each pop punishes the dog for not being in the appropriate position. But one pop is often followed by another if the dog does not immediately assume perfect heel position, and so he is popped for forging, popped for lagging, popped for being too wide or too close. He is given lots of information about what *not* to do, but told precious little about what he *should* do to escape the pops. Although eventually, through a process of elimination (or sheer luck), the dog may learn correct heel position, this does not happen before he has been thoroughly indoctrinated against heeling. And dogs often generalize this fear or dislike to all obedience training.

The Importance of Clarity

Although experiments have established conclusively that punishment is effective in suppressing targeted behavior, there are many problems inherent in its application. If a punishment is to be effective, it must be clear to the dog which behavior is being punished. This means that the punishment must be delivered *immediately* after that behavior. Any delay reduces the value of the punishment and creates confusion in the dog's mind, since other behaviors may have occurred between the behavior that was intended to be punished and the punishment itself.

Suppose I have a dominant male dog who feels the need to leave his personal mark in the obedience ring. As he lifts his leg, I start towards him to punish the behavior. But before I can get to him, he sees me coming and trots over to meet me. If I punish him at this point, I will be punishing him for coming to me, not for his marking behavior. It is very difficult to administer a timely punishment for behaviors that occur at some distance from the trainer or for behaviors that are totally unexpected. Effective punishment necessitates careful planning and precisely defined opportunities.

Other Problems with Punishment

In addition, it is difficult (for both dogs and people) to generalize many punishments beyond the particular environments in which they occur.

Children who are punished at home for socially unacceptable behaviors do not suppress these behaviors very well outside the home or away from their punisher unless the punishment can be administered in all the different environments and without the obvious presence of the punisher. Most of us know dogs who would not dream of raiding the garbage when the owner is at home, but who become trash-eating demons in the owner's absence.

Another problem with punishment is that it tends to suppress behaviors other than the one it intends to eliminate. Dogs who are punished frequently will often refuse to offer even behaviors that are rewarded. Punishment may destroy the confidence that is necessary for the successful competition dog and may make him feel helpless to control what happens to him. When a dog shuts down and refuses to offer any behaviors at all, he is telling us that he would rather do nothing than be wrong, or that he believes he is powerless to do anything that is right.

This is not to say that punishment should never be used. There are times when punishment may be necessary to save your dog's life. It may be the only safe and sure way to eliminate a behavior, and some dogs engage in behaviors that make them impossible to live with. Dogs that exhibit inappropriate social behaviors, such as biting people or attacking other dogs, must be stopped. And the strong point of punishment is that, if administered correctly, it can almost immediately eliminate the behavior at which it is aimed.

In my part of the country, dogs that chase deer are shot with no questions asked. I once house-sat for friends, and as part of the deal I took on the care and training of their pet Borzoi, Kyah. Their house was on the edge of a lovely quiet woods, networked with paths for walking. Kyah and I had a wonderful time until a deer popped into view. Off she went, heedless to my calls. I now faced a difficult decision. I could leave Kyah at home during these walks, teach her that chasing deer was off limits, or risk having my friends return to a Borzoi-less house. Finally I gritted my teeth, borrowed a shock collar, read the instructions carefully, and used the collar. Kyah was punished by a shock the instant she took a step after a fleeing deer. Because the collar applied punishment precisely and at the right time, and Kyah was not stupid, she abandoned her pursuit of deer in a matter of days. As distasteful as the idea of shocking a dog was, I found the image of a dog confined without the opportunity to run even more unpleasant. In this case, the punishment was worth it (and I think Kyah would have agreed).

> ## The Bottom Line
> "Punishment is a difficult and unpleasant technique for modifying behavior. It is almost never sufficient by itself. At best, it eliminates the target behavior, but when it does so, it leaves a kind of behavioral vacuum, and some other behavior will come along and fill [it]. . . Unless the individual possesses a repertoire of behaviors that are effective and adaptive, there is no reason to assume that what arises to fill the vacuum will be an improvement on what it is replacing. So something more than punishment, like shaping using positive reinforcement, is required. But there is no denying that punishment is effective. And it is effective quickly. In situations in which rapid and dramatic change is essential, there may be no substitute for punishment."[1]

Guidelines for the Effective Administration of Punishment

If you have determined that punishment is necessary, here is a quick checklist for its effective application.

1. The punishment should be intense. This probably contradicts what most of you have been told at training school. The common wisdom is that the trainer should apply the least amount of pain necessary. But this is one of the places where laboratory experiments have proved the dog trainer wrong. If we want our punishments to be maximally effective — to work quickly and to last for a long period of time — they must not be so mild that they have to be repeated on an escalating scale to be effective.

Dogs easily become acclimated to gradually increasing degrees of discomfort. The trainer who starts at a low level and works up will find herself applying a much harsher punishment to her dog in the long run than the trainer who administers a more severe punishment at the first occurrence of the unwanted behavior. A dog that is initially exposed to a mild aversive develops a tolerance to that aversive and to the gradually increasing degrees of pain administered thereafter. The dog that is severely corrected has no such chance to adapt. The punishment therefore makes a far stronger impression on him, and he is likely to change his behavior immediately. Further, it is less likely that the behavior will recur later.

---

[1]B. Schwartz, S. Robbins. *Learning and Operant Behavior*, W.W. Norton & Co., 1995, p.243

2. Punishment should be delivered unemotionally. Most of us do not want to punish our dogs. Frequently, we resort to punishing only when we have exhausted all other strategies. Trainers who have reached this point are often emotionally frustrated with their lack of success and with their dogs. A trainer who waits to punish her dog until his behaviors have made her angry, or one who cannot bring herself to punish until she is emotionally involved, confuses and frightens the dog by her emotional reaction. A confused dog has a much more difficult time processing the information that the punishment is intended to convey than a dog who is confronted with a punishment delivered without emotion. Regardless of how good it might make the trainer feel to vent her anger, punishment should never be delivered in the spirit of revenge. The only appropriate function of punishment is that of eliminating a behavior — it is not a trainer catharsis.

In addition, when emotion enters the picture, it is easy for punishment to become abuse. If possible, determine prior to the training session just what behavior needs to be eliminated and how severe the punishment will be. Bear in mind that, regardless of the nature of the punishment or the negative reinforcement, aversives are only effective if they are administered correctly. An apologetic trainer who really does not want to punish the dog or a trainer who has been pushed over the edge into anger cannot administer an aversive that gives valuable information to the dog.

3. The punishment should be delivered immediately. The longer the delay, the greater the number of intervening behaviors and the less informative the punishment. A punishment must be understood to be effective.

4. The punishment should be consistent. Remember that the behavior that is being punished has been reinforced by something in the environment, and to allow the behavior to go unpunished is to allow it to continue to be reinforced. Therefore, if you only punish sometimes, you are placing the punished behavior on a variable schedule of reinforcement. On the occasions when you don't punish the dog for the behavior, he is being reinforced for the undesirable behavior, and a variable schedule of reinforcement is the one that most strongly resists extinction.

5. The punishment should signal that reinforcement for the punished behavior is not available. If, for example, you are going to punish your dog for getting into the garbage, he should know that the garbage is not going to be there after he is punished. And he must not be allowed to gulp his mouthful down before he is punished. Whatever had been reinforcing the unwanted behavior must be removed from the picture.

6. Provide an analogous behavior that is an acceptable means to reinforcement. If your dog seeks affection by flinging himself upon strangers, you might teach him that by sitting nicely, he will be reinforced with affectionate pats by guests, thus eliminating the need for him to engage in jumping.

The Difference Between Punishment and Negative Reinforcement

There is a great deal of confusion about the difference between punishment and negative reinforcement, and it is easy to understand why. Remember that negative reinforcement involves the *removal* of an aversive stimulus. For the stimulus to be removed, it first must be applied. Positive punishment is the addition of an aversive stimulus. In fact, sometimes, in order to be able to have a negative reinforcement, you must first have a positive punishment.

For example, many people use a bark breaker to silence dogs that are incessant barkers. The bark breaker is triggered by the sound of a dog barking, and it emits a loud and (to canine ears) very unpleasant sound. The sound represents the *addition* of an aversive stimulus (and is therefore positive). It is a punishment because it occurs after a behavior and is intended to *eliminate* it. But when the dog stops barking, the bark breaker turns itself off. Thus, the *removal* of the sound is also a negative reinforcer for silence. No wonder there is confusion!

Although proper scientific use of the words does not always matter, it is important to understand the differences between punishment and negative reinforcement because of how each functions. If you intend to negatively reinforce a behavior, but inadvertently apply the aversive stimulus at the wrong time, you may end up punishing, and thus eliminating the behavior. The following is a training example that demonstrates this difference.

Punishment and Negative Reinforcement — An Example

Suppose you normally practice with your dog in an enclosed area with no distractions. Your training sessions almost always go well, and both you and the dog enjoy them greatly. But the dog learns to recognize the signs that the session is about to end, and he refuses to come when called after you have picked up the training gear and are ready to leave. You know that the dog understands that he should come when called and that his reluctance to leave is caused by his anticipation of the end of the fun training session. But you are also worried that this disobedience might spill over into other situations in which the dog would prefer to do something other than to come to you. Although you have reinforced the dog with all kinds of good treats for coming, these alone do not seem sufficient to produce a reliable recall for such times. You decide to shoot all of your training ammunition at this problem. You want to positively and negatively reinforce the dog when he comes and to punish him for refusal to come. Table 4.1 shows one way to break all these different responses out.

Table 4.1. Reinforcement Versus Punishment

	Positive	**Negative**
Reinforcement	Praise, treat after behavior.	Gentle pressure on lead is released as the dog comes.
Punishment	Use a series of short pops to correct the dog towards you after he refuses to come.	Pack up your gear, get into the car and leave after the dog refuses to come.

Row 1 describes positive and negative reinforcement. To positively reinforce a correct recall, you would offer an appetitive stimulus after the behavior occurs. You would tell your pal that he is wonderful and give him a treat. To negatively reinforce the recall, you would put a long line on the dog and exert gentle pressure on the line as you call the dog. The pressure of the line is an aversive stimulus. As the dog begins to move in your direction, the pressure on the line releases. This is reinforcing since the elimination of the aversive stimulus reinforces the dog to offer the behavior that canceled it.

Row 2 deals with punishment. What you are seeking to eliminate is the refusal of the dog to come. When punishment is the intent, application of an aversive stimulus should follow the behavior it seeks to eliminate. Therefore, once you call the dog and he pays no attention, you would immediately introduce a punishment. To punish positively, you would add an aversive stimulus. You might, for example, have a friend toss a throw can (a can containing pebbles or coins) behind the dog, or you might walk over to the dog, attach his leash, and bring him to you with a series of short collar pops all the way. The noise of the can and the collar pops are aversive stimuli. To apply a negative punishment, you would remove an appetitive stimulus from the environment. In this environment, *you* are probably the most appetitive stimulus for your dog. So you might remove yourself, or pretend to do so, from the situation by pretending to pack up and go home.

Your aim is to convince the dog that failure to come results in unpleasant consequences (punishment) and that coming, even if it does signify the end of the training session, both aborts the negative results and produces positive ones (negative and positive reinforcement).

Why Use Aversives At All?

Trainers who refuse to use aversives usually do so because they fear aversives will affect the attitude of the dog or destroy his motivation. They believe that the use of aversive stimuli may impair their relationship with the dog, a relationship on which the competition performance might depend. They fear that their dogs might come to dislike all training, or worse, come to associate the trainers themselves with pain and suffering. No aversives, they argue, are worth that!

They are right — if all applications of aversive stimuli have these negative consequences. But aversives do not have to have negative consequences. Many trainers who use both aversive and appetitive stimuli have shown that aversives need not demotivate, need not impair the relationship, but can add to the dog's understanding of appropriate behaviors.

Aversives as a Natural Part of Life

In order to survive in nature, animals depend on information provided by aversive stimuli. Excessive cold teaches the animal to seek life-sustaining warmth, hunger pangs tell him to eat, and thirst causes him to drink. Our puppies are exposed to aversives before their eyes open and before they can hear. Take a pup and move him away from his mother's warm body. See how quickly the discomfort of the lowered temperature causes him to work his way back. Bitches routinely correct pups that are biting too hard with a snarl, a snap, or a quick shake. The pups don't reject their mothers. Indeed, they learn a valuable lesson in how to relate to other members of their pack.

Chances are that when you brought your own little pup home, he engaged in behaviors that were less than desirable. You probably used some sort of aversive stimulus like a loud clap of the hands or a tap on the nose to tell him not to chew on the couch, eat the garbage, or jump on the baby. Unless you were excessively harsh or did not show the puppy clearly what he should not do, your pup did not love you less for it, and you certainly did not destroy his desire to be a member of the family. Aversives furnish the dog with vital information he needs in order to be a member of both his canine and his human packs. In the long run, the puppy's life is more secure and happy because he was taught all the rules of the game right from the start.

Aversives in Training

Since aversives function effectively and non-destructively in dogs' lives outside of training sessions, there is no reason why they can't be used with similar effects in training. Regardless of whether a dog is to be trained for the performance ring or for family life, it is important for him to understand the commands his trainer gives. One of them just might save his life!

What does the trainer really intend to tell the dog when commanding him, for example, to come? She is not saying, "Come to me unless there is something else you would rather do." In most cases, the command is not optional. It means "Come now, regardless of what else you find enticing." Those who see a role for aversives in training argue that the circle of obedience communication is incomplete until the dog understands that commands are not a matter of choice. These trainers also argue that dogs who understand this, who are responsible for all of their actions, can be happy, motivated, and able to obey commands with willingness and enjoyment. If the dog understands what aversives mean and how to eliminate them, he remains in control of the situation. It is this comprehension and control that builds positive attitude and consistent performance.

In addition, they argue, dogs who do not understand aversives, who are only trained with appetitive stimuli, are unreliable in many performance venues. A dog who has been taught to offer a behavior only because he desires the consequences of that behavior may consider the consequences of other behaviors more desirable on any given day. On a very hot day, it may be more comfortable for him to leave the heat of the sun in the obedience ring and seek the shade of the judge's table. In his own mind, he has done nothing wrong since he has been taught to work for appetitive stimuli. I received the following letter from a training correspondent. It demonstrates the fallacy of training without aversives:

> "Help! I thought I had done everything right! I taught the exercises positively, put the dog on a schedule of variable reinforcement, lengthened the periods between reinforcements, and repeated the same gradual process when I went to matches. I started by doing a lot of feeding and went to variable rein-forcement there, too. I thought I was ready to show! But I went to a match yesterday for a dress rehearsal, and it was a DISAS-TER!!! The dog was awful. NO attention, sloppy heeling, lousy recall. I looked at the other end of my leash and didn't recog-nize the dog there! What did I do wrong??"

I could have written this very letter to myself, for I experienced ex-actly the same thing with my dog, Bear.

Bear's Dress Rehearsal
I honestly thought Bear was ready for her obedience ring debut. She had been well trained, proofed, and extensively matched. I had tried to make all aspects of her training positive and upbeat. I then took her to one last match as kind of a dress rehearsal for the real thing. It was a hot day and Bear and I didn't enter the ring until after noon. I should have known that bad things were about to happen when I gave her the 'watch' command and she only briefly glanced up at my face before she gazed dreamily away at a nearby pond. Bear's performance was awful! She was so busy gawking around that she had no idea where I was or where we were going. During the heeling she bumped, banged, and crowded on the inside turns, and lagged and went wide on the outside ones. Changes of pace were nonexistent! Although she did come to me on the recall, she made no attempt to give me a straight front or finish. To top it all off, she decided she did not want to lie down on the down stay, and when I took her collar and tried to push her down, she growled. I could imagine the comments of the spectators: " Surely she should know better than to show a dog who is so untrained!"

It was a long drive home. How I agonized over that match. What had I done wrong? Bear knew those exercises; she had performed them in all sorts of different environments and at many matches with no reinforcement in the ring. I had done everything I knew of to insure that my dog was confident and secure in the exercises. Was there something I had not done? The only thing I had neglected to do in these different environments was to administer aversives when Bear offered less than satisfactory performances. I had asked her to try again, and I had helped her through exercises she seemed to be weak on, but I had not told her, "Don't do that!"

Why Aversives are Important

Bear's performance taught me a valuable lesson! I now believe that the failure to show the dog what not to do deprives the dog of information the team needs to be successful in the performance ring. Yes, the dog understands that he will be reinforced if he performs the requested behavior. But someday there will be a more powerful reinforcement available. A child walking by eating an ice cream cone, a bitch in season, all that nice shade under the tree just outside the ring. And, in lieu of being told that it is not permissible to seek the greener grass, why should the dog not pursue stronger reinforcements?

Coupled with the *possibility* of competing reinforcements in any performance venue is the *certainty* that once you embark on a show career with your dog you may never offer food or toys to the dog while he is performing. Although you may fool him for awhile by going to matches and feeding and playing there, the seasoned competition dog knows that there are times when food is not available. Successful competition dogs are willing to work anyway. Why? Partly because the exercises themselves are positively reinforcing, and partly because working with the handler has become a strong conditioned reinforcer. In addition, the dog has been taught that compliance with the handler's commands is not optional. This is the part of Bear's education that I had neglected.

Completing the Circle

It is very important to fill in all the blanks before you too have an experience like Bear and I had. It is critical to teach the dog that he is responsible for all of his behaviors, not just those that please him. Indeed, some of us may have inadvertently taught our dogs that failure to comply actually was fun. The trainer who runs out to the dumbbell after her dog refuses to retrieve it may show the dog that refusal to obey a retrieve command results in a fun game. The trainer who simply waits for the inattentive dog to look back and then rewards him for so doing may be teaching the dog that looking away is the beginning of the food chain. Certainly we do not want to introduce exercises to our dogs in a painful way, but just as certainly we do not want to be unclear about our expectation that a dog obey regardless of competing stimuli. Aversives convey this information very well indeed if they are clearly and fairly administered.

Good trainers may even administer corrections occasionally in a formal ring performance and sacrifice a passing or even a winning score to show the dog that his behavior is unacceptable. One of the best trainers I know was showing an excellent Border Collie in the obedience Utility class. The dog was working a lovely class but was also taking advantage of the formal environment. On each finish, as he circled behind her, he would quickly lower his head and sniff the ground. He was a fast worker, and to the audience, his finishes seemed more than acceptable in terms of speed. But his trainer was not satisfied and became increasingly suspicious that something was slowing the dog down. Finally she gave the command to finish and whirled just as the dog lowered his head for his quick sniff. "Stop that!" she said, and the dog looked up in surprise. The judge shook his head sadly and said, "You just blew first place," and excused her from the ring (as he should have done). The trainer was not at all sorry. She was happy to trade a class placement for a chance to give her dog some much needed ring information. "He won't be sniffing in the ring for a long while," she said in satisfaction.

Most dogs who are confident in their abilities and who have been given the opportunity to understand what the correct behavior is will profit from the information aversives furnish. These dogs gain understanding from corrections and do not lose motivation. Application of aversive stimuli to dogs who have been well and positively trained are simply an additional means of communication. If the training foundations are solid, the dog already has a good attitude about you and training, and he can certainly benefit from the added information. Aversives need not be harsh or painful, and if the handler takes care to communicate to the dog exactly what they mean, they need not be applied frequently.

Aversive Education

It is very important that you teach your dog exactly what aversives mean and how he can avoid them by either offering acceptable behaviors or ceasing undesirable ones. Although puppies learn how to avoid or escape the aversives that come from other dogs, aversives applied by humans can be frightening and confusing. For example, if a punishment does not immediately follow a behavior, the dog may make no connection between his actions and

the consequences. Many of the behaviors we teach our dogs for the performance ring are not behaviors they offer naturally. Part of our job is to teach
our dogs what aversives mean in terms of those behaviors. They need to know
why the aversives are being administered and what makes them go away.

Three Dog Stories

Kryssie is a Soft-Coated Wheaten Terrier — dominant, bright, and
very energetic. Hershey is a chocolate Lab and is a fanatic retriever. Amber
was a rough Collie, intelligent and very soft. These dogs provide fascinating
illustrations about the nature of training with aversive and appetitive stimuli.

Kryssie

When Kryssie had been heeling nicely for over a year, her trainer,
Betsy, decided it might be time to consider entering her in an obedience trial.
Betsy originally had been introduced to dog training by a professional trainer
who believed in using only aversives. After she saw the effects on her dogs of
exclusive use of aversives, Betsy converted to positive training with enthusiasm, and had been training Kryssie with only appetitive stimuli — food and
toys. Although Kryssie had been put on a variable schedule of reinforcement,
she had never done a food-free run-through, and one night Betsy decided to
see how Kryssie would do in that situation. She took off her bait bag and had
me call a heeling pattern for them.

To our mutual surprise, Kryssie was awful! Her attention disappeared
at exactly the same time the food did! I told Betsy that Kryssie knew how to
heel and was choosing not to comply. "She needs to know that she *has* to heel
when you ask her," I said, and I told Betsy to give the dog some mild collar
pops on a buckle collar. Despite these, Kryssie lagged and sniffed her way
through the whole first part of the heeling pattern before we mercifully called
a halt. We agreed that Kryssie had to learn that attention was not optional. So
we put a prong collar on the dog and again gently corrected her for her inat-
tention. Although it was very clear that Kryssie hated the corrections, her
responses were not at all what we had expected. Instead of complying with
Betsy's demands for attention, Kryssie fought the corrections in every way she
could (Fig. 4.2). She lunged forward, lagged behind, and finally refused to
budge at all. In frustration, we put the dog away and tried to figure out exactly
what had happened.

Hershey

Before we could resolve that situation, I found myself confronting a similar problem with a very different dog and handler. Hershey's owner, Elaine, was a student in my Beginning Open obedience class who had been training Hershey, her first dog, positively from the start. A true Labrador Retriever, Hershey loved to retrieve and had been taught to do so positively (not that she needed much teaching). Although I believe in introducing a retrieve positively, I also believe that, for a dog to be genuinely solid on retrieving, he must be shown what will happen should he choose to refuse to retrieve. To do this, some kind of aversive stimulus must be administered and it must be done in a carefully controlled situation.

Like the other dogs in Elaine's class, Hershey had been taught what a retrieve was, and she had positive associations with the dumbbell. Therefore, I felt it was time to introduce an element of compulsion to the retrieve exercise. I spent fully two hours with the class showing them how to use various forms of compulsion in a way that made sense to the dogs. Although Elaine was fearful that application of an aversive stimulus would hurt the dog's attitude, she agreed that it needed to be done. The next night she sat with the dog in her living room and tossed the dumbbell in front of the dog. Then she tossed a piece of food next to the dumbbell. On the command, "Take it," Hershey chose the food and Elaine applied an aversive stimulus. Instead of picking up the dumbbell, Hershey chose to leave. Pulling loose from Elaine, she ran from the room and refused to even look at the dumbbell for the rest of the night. Elaine was devastated, and her husband didn't help when he said, "Stop torturing the dog."

Elaine contacted me just two nights after my experience with Betsy and Kryssie. Both trainers were understandably worried that the application of aversive stimuli had destroyed their dogs' attitudes — attitudes that they had carefully nurtured for the whole of their dogs' lives. Although I was sure that this was not the case, I was puzzled that the application of relatively mild aversives should have elicited such extreme reactions from both dogs. And then I remembered Amber.

Amber

On the surface, Amber's story seems to be the opposite of the other two dogs. Amber was my first dog, a dog trained totally with aversives (standard technique twenty years ago in my area). Although Amber learned all of

Victoria A. Dale

Fig. 4.2. Kryssie was trained using no aversives. When her trainer then corrected her for lagging (left), Kryssie fought them (right).

the obedience exercises very rapidly, her ring performances were not pretty. She lagged and dragged her way around the ring, and I allowed myself to be convinced that it was her breed and not her training that was responsible for those performances. One night I saw a demonstration given by a woman who trained her dogs with food. This was considered a bizarre and exotic method at that time. Her Dobermans worked with speed and enjoyment. One even leapt into her arms at the end of an exercise! Perhaps, I reasoned, food was an answer to Amber's plodding performances. Perhaps I could replace the death march *Broad Jump* front with a joyful leap. Amber did love food (I knew that for sure), so I went home and broke out the hot dogs. Not only did Amber like the food, she went crazy for it! She abandoned all vestiges of training in her frantic attempts to get at the hot dogs. She pushed and leapt and bounced wildly in front of me. She was oblivious to my demands that she heel. In fact, she seemed totally unable to hear any of my commands in her frenzy to get her teeth on those hot dogs (Fig. 4.3). So I gave up on using food. It had seemed a good idea at the time, but it obviously made my dog too crazy.

What made me connect Amber's story with those of the other two dogs was her wildly inappropriate responses to stimuli. In this she was similar to both Kryssie and Hershey, who also had exhibited extreme responses to

Fig. 4.3. When Amber was first introduced to food in training, she was so excited that she forgot all of her commands.

stimuli, even though those stimuli were negative whereas Amber's were positive. Why did these stimuli produce such overreactions by what were, after all, well-trained dogs?

My hypothesis is that, although all three trainers had intended the application of the stimuli to be informative, the dogs had perceived them as totally meaningless. They had never encountered these stimuli in all of their experience, and the stimuli were thus perceived as nonsensical — they were not part of what the dogs had come to expect in the training context.

All operant conditioning rests upon the principle of association — the primary principle of **classical conditioning**.

> For a stimulus to be an effective training device, the dog must be able to **associate** the stimulus with the response.

What was missing for these three dogs was an understanding of the behavior that would have enabled them to control the situation. Simply, none of these dogs understood that it was they who, by their own actions could make the aversives go away or the appetitives appear. All three believed that there was no connection between their behaviors and environmental events.

Kryssie and Hershey had been trained with only appetitive stimuli; they had never experienced anything aversive in the training context. Although they understood that they could produce the appetitive stimuli by their own actions, they had no understanding that the aversives were also caused by their actions or that the aversives could be removed by further actions. Amber's case was the opposite of the other two. She had been trained with aversives, and she knew how to remove them. But she had never been trained with appetitives and had no idea how to make them happen again. All three dogs had lost control of their respective training situations. It makes sense that their first response was to revert to more natural ways of either avoiding or obtaining stimuli. Kryssie and Hershey tried to abandon the situation, either by fighting or fleeing. Amber tried to obtain the goodies in the good old fashioned doggie way, by poking, prodding, and otherwise forcing me to give them up. None of the dogs understood that they were still in training mode and that they could produce the desired results simply by offering the behavior requested by their trainers.

The solution to such a situation is not for the trainer to abandon application of the relevant stimuli. Betsy and Elaine should not go back to feeding exclusively. And, were Amber still alive, I would go and get the hot dogs out again. The solution is to work the dog through his confusion, to help the dog learn the association between his actions and the stimuli so that he can regain control of the situation. These three dogs taught me that the sudden introduction of stimuli, whether appetitive or aversive, must be accompanied by information that shows the dog how to cope with those stimuli.

Learned Helplessness

If a trainer does not take the time to help the dog understand how to cope with aversives, the results can be damaging indeed. The phenomenon of **learned helplessness** illustrates what happens when an animal is unable to understand the connection between its actions and the occurrence of environmental stimuli. The following is a classical experiment that demonstrates what happens when an animal is convinced that it has no control whatsoever over its situation. (Please bear in mind that this experiment was conducted many years ago and would not be permitted today.)

Experimenters placed dogs in boxes divided into two parts by a low barrier. The dogs were taught to avoid an electric shock applied to the floor of one side of the partition by jumping to the other side. The dogs were then yoked together in pairs and placed in a situation in which the responses of only one of the dogs controlled the delivery of shock. That is, one dog received a shock regardless of what he did, while the other was able to terminate the current for both by climbing over the partition. After several of these experiences, the dogs were unyoked and individually placed in a divided room in which they could again avoid a shock by jumping a hurdle. While the dogs that controlled the stimuli in the yoked experiment easily learned the new behavior (as did dogs with no previous experimental experience), the member of the yoked pair that had no previous control over the situation made no attempt to escape the situation. Although clearly frightened by the repeated shocks, those dogs initially whined and panted uneasily. As the experiment progressed, they became more and more passive, finally lying down and offering almost no motion at all in response to shocks.

The dogs that had no way to control the delivery of the shock had developed learned helplessness. They had come to believe that environmental events were independent of their actions. This belief interfered with their attempts to control anything that happened to them. They would not even attempt to flee a threatening environment. These dogs had been taught to be helpless — that no matter what they did, their actions would not produce significant consequences. When the helpless dogs were then helped over the hurdles by the experimenters a number of times, they eventually were able to be taught to again make the appropriate responses. Thus, helplessness can be both learned and unlearned.

> To prevent learned helplessness, you must teach your dog how to escape the aversive and how to prevent it from happening again .

Timing — When to Introduce Aversives

It is probably best to introduce aversives early in training. Remember that dogs come with some prior experiences of aversives even if those experiences were limited to maternal corrections in the whelping box. Your dog's initial exposure to aversives need not involve severe discomfort. Indeed, should take the time to teach your dog how to handle aversives before using them to perfect an exercise. The message that aversives give must be clear, and the dog must be taught how to regain control of the situation (Fig. 4.4). Applications of aversives at the early stage of training will make it easier for the dog to understand the conditions under which he is expected to work. Thus, the information furnished by the aversives is valuable indeed. In fact, early introduction may actually enhance the dog's ability to control his situation.

The Dangers of Delay

Unfortunately, many trainers do not see a need to use aversives in training until the dog moves out of familiar situations; they wait until the dog begins to be exposed to match or show situations where his attention may be distracted by the novelty of the environment. At this stage of training, it is easy for the trainer, who has invested a great deal of time and energy in the endeavor, to become discouraged in the results of her positive training and disappointed in the dog. In addition, there is a new sense of urgency because the competition is approaching. As a result, there is a tendency to rush the dog's exposure to the new aversive stimuli and to substitute greater and greater degrees of discomfort for the time and patience necessary to acclimatize the dog to unfamiliar stimuli. Further, because the trainer is stressed by the pressure of having entered shows for which she feels her dog is not ready and is disappointed in the inefficacy of her initial training efforts, her

Victoria A. Dale

Fig. 4.4. The dog should have a clear idea of how to avoid the aversive. In this case, by lying down, the dog can stop the downward pressure on his collar.

emotions may creep into the administration of aversives. This can interfere with the dog's ability to process information.

Introduction of and education about aversive control is far better done in low stress training sessions in familiar environments. Regardless of the training method, switching gears immediately before a show confuses the dog and can even ruin a show career. The dog may very well associate the newly introduced aversives with the show or match conditions and may never again feel comfortable in that environment.

From the dog's point of view, delaying the onset of stimuli, whether aversive or appetitive, until late into his training career may amount to changing the rules. Worse, it may create learned helplessness, making the dog believe that his behavior no longer has environmental results. The confusion and stress of having to understand a new set of rules at this late stage may destroy much of the confidence so carefully built by the trainer. Undoing the damage at this point may take longer than if a variety of aversives had been carefully introduced much earlier in the dog's career.

5. In Search of Excellence

The Principle:
THE TEAM FACTOR

The ultimate goal of the competition dog trainer is to have the dog understand what is expected of him so thoroughly that he can offer a credible performance in any environment. Perfect scores in your own backyard gain no titles and win no prizes. Even if you are training house manners, it's far more convenient to have a dog who is willing to obey on visits and vacations as well as at home (Fig. 5.1).

Too many dog trainers believe that the transfer of a behavior from one environment to another should be automatic; they expect that if their dogs understand and comply with commands at home, it should be no special task for him to offer similar behaviors elsewhere.

But, in fact, this is not true. Remember how frightening you found your first days at school? Or how hard it was to adjust to college life during your freshman year? And what about stage fright, when all those lines you spent weeks and months learning suddenly flew right out of your head as soon as you looked out over the footlights? The first time I stepped into the obedience ring my knees were shaking so hard I almost couldn't walk, and my voice came out in a croak. No matter how much we practice, no matter how well we memorize behaviors, a change in environment can radically interfere with our ability to offer them. Likewise, changes in the environment affect your dog's ability to offer even the most solidly grounded behaviors. They may even make him appear totally untrained.

Fig. 5.1. The ultimate goal of obedience training is to have a dog that can perform well in a variety of environments.

Operant conditioning can never be the exact science for the dog trainer that it is for the laboratory scientist. In the laboratory, virtually all environmental conditions are controlled, from the temperature to the physical structure of the cage to the genetic makeup of the experimental animals. This makes it far easier for the scientist to observe and predict animal behaviors because the animals are not affected by unpredictable changes in the environment. It is a different story for our dogs, who are constantly exposed to changing locations, spectators, applause, and the presence of other animals. Even marine mammals don't take their show on the road — their audiences come to them. Because of this, dog trainers face a more difficult task than trainers who have a greater degree of environmental control.

Environmental Variables

There are two main types of environmental variables that affect dogs' performances. First, there is the internal state of the dog — its instincts and physical and psychological condition on any given day. Second, and equally important, is the external physical environment — whether the dog is being asked to perform in familiar, safe surroundings or ones that may be perceived as hostile.

Internal Variables

The internal environment includes factors like your dog's natural drives and instincts. For example, my Border Collie, Coe, is absolutely unable to pay attention to obedience commands when sheep are around. His herding instinct acts as a block to all other environmental stimuli. Although he often has offered class-winning obedience performances in the absence of livestock, let him hear one sheep, and both the obedience ring and me cease to exist for him. I have seen a wonderful Welsh Springer Spaniel with a Tracking Dog Excellent title suddenly abandon his track simply because a bird flew up in front of him (Fig. 5.2) and a West Highland White Terrier abandon a class-winning performance to explore a gap at the back of the ring in the certainty that it sheltered vermin.

Instincts can also have a positive effect on a dog's ability to perform. Most retrievers love to fetch dumbbells and thus are easily reinforced in the obedience ring. The sight of a fast-moving target incites sight hounds to put every ounce of speed they have into the chase, and any self-respecting Border Collie would be insulted if his trainer offered treats for an excellent job of herding. The more you know about your breed and its proclivities, the more you should be able to capitalize upon those traits that contribute to your performance sport and to guard against those that might interfere.

Fig. 5.2. Instincts can interfere with performance. A low-flying bird made this Welsh Springer Spaniel forget about his track.

Just as there are breed-related variables that affect performance, there are also variables associated with the individual dog that can influence the quality of performance. Trainers need to pay attention to these. Many a dog, initially accused of being disobedient, was later diagnosed as having a physical injury that made some behaviors painful. The dog's health is an internal variable that should always be considered when a dog suddenly stops offering a learned behavior.

Individual dogs may have quirks that a good trainer can capitalize on. My Border Collie, Mikey, loves to lick my face (something I find very distasteful). Although I do not allow him any doggie kisses during the course of our normal lives, in the obedience ring between exercises, I will often let him give me a big slurpy kiss to keep him up and happy (Fig. 5.3).

External Variables

One of the things that most differentiates us from our dogs is the significance of language. Humans have come to rely on the written and spoken word as the major source of information about the environment. If we want to go somewhere, we read a map or write a set of directions. If we want to make a cake, we use a recipe. I clearly remember my Aunt Clara refusing to believe a storm was coming, even as the dark clouds approached and thunder rumbled, because the weather report said it would be dry and sunny.

Dogs do not attach nearly as much importance to the spoken word. They are much more like their ancestors, animals that relied on changes in the environment for information vital to their survival. What you say to your dog is far less important than how you say it. "What a wonderful dog you are," delivered by a person towering intimidatingly over a dog will send him scurrying for cover. For the dog, body language is far more significant than words, and physical surroundings provide far more information than all the news and weather reports in the world.

Dogs that are routinely trained in one or two places come to accept their training environments as safe places. Because the physical surroundings remain the same, the dog need not devote any attention to them. He is free to concentrate entirely on his trainer and the exercises he is asked to perform. But even in this secure environment a dog will check out minor variations — the addition of a new jump or a neighborhood child hanging over the fence to watch, for instance.

Fig. 5.3. Individual dogs have quirks (like enjoying a slurpy lick) that a good trainer uses to advantage.

Change the environment radically and your dog's behavior usually changes, too. When a dog is taken to a new location, his behavior is usually less polished. Much of this loss of proficiency is due to a loss of focus. The dog has transferred his attention from you and the behaviors he is being asked to perform to the novelty of the different venue. This is normal and natural, and it is important that you help your dog get acclimated to working in many different environments.

Environmental Control

One strategy for dealing with deterioration in trained behaviors in response to the environment is to control the training environment. Since dogs attach such great importance to their surroundings, it is helpful if you duplicate the ring environment in your training sessions as much as possible. If you are planning to campaign your dog in obedience and you can afford it, it helps tremendously to make your training area look like an obedience ring. Set up baby gates or other ring barriers that are used in your area, and arrange the jumps the way they often are in the formal ring. The goal is for the dog to then walk into the competition venue and feel at home. The more things he finds familiar, the less he will have to pay attention to anything but you. Attention to detail is very important — animals are extremely attentive to even slight

111

environmental variations. Studies have repeatedly shown that animals are more likely to respond correctly in environments that are familiar to them.

Discriminative Stimuli

Many years ago, I noticed that my Collie, Amber, would get very excited whenever I took off my work shoes. She would become even more excited when I went to the closet and got out my hiking boots. By the time I had them laced and tied, the entire apartment rang with her barks of delight and anticipation. Since I am reasonably sure that Amber did not have a hiking boot fixation, it is clear that those boots became meaningful for her because she had come to associate them with our walks in the woods. The appearance of the hiking boots signaled to her that something enjoyable was about to happen. I have also noticed that opening the drawer of the bureau in which I keep the toenail clippers precipitates the disappearance of every dog I own.

Changes in the environment signal important things to animals. In particular, they give information about the availability of appetitives or aversives. For Amber, the sight of the hiking shoes signaled the coming of a walk; for my current dogs, the sound of the opening drawer signals the ordeal of toenail clipping. Wild animals need such signals in order to survive. Thus, the hare runs at the sound of rustling grass, and the deer flees at the sound of the gun. In their minds, these sounds are associated with danger. The technical name for these events is **discriminative stimuli**.

Let's look at two common examples of discriminative stimuli. In the obedience Novice class, the team must perform two heeling exercises, one on leash and the other off leash. Although many dogs do both exercises in similar ways, the behavior of some dogs radically changes once the leash is removed. Commonly, the heeling performance degenerates when the leash is taken off. Dogs that maintained correct heel position during the on-leash portion of the exercise lag behind their handlers, go wide on turns and, in extreme cases, refuse to heel at all. These dogs have come to associate the presence of the leash with the availability of aversives. In training, if they lagged or went wide, they were corrected with a leash pop. If they made a mistake off-leash, their trainers put the leash back on and administered aversives for incorrect behaviors. If the only incentive to heel well is a threat that the dog will be punished if he doesn't, then the removal of the threat of punishment also removes the necessity for the behavior.

Another example deals with the availability of appetitives. Many trainers tie bait bags around their waists so that food will be readily available. Although they may wean their dogs gradually from most treats during a training session, they continue to wear the bag so that when they do reward, they can do it quickly. Their dogs offer the trained behaviors in part because the bait bag signals that reinforcement is possible. However, when the trainer enters the competition ring, she cannot bring any food. If her dog has come to depend on the presence of the bait bag as a signal that he will be reinforced, its absence may indicate to him that reinforcement is no longer possible (Fig. 5.4). If he has been trained to work only for food reinforcement, he may abandon the previously well-trained behaviors.

Two Important Applications

Cue words should function as discriminative stimuli. If I tell my dog to sit and he does, I will reinforce him. When he sits on other occasions, in the absence of a cue, he shouldn't expect to be reinforced. In the obedience ring, a dog is awarded a passing score only if he offers the required behaviors on command. Dogs that retrieve before they're commanded receive the same

Victoria A. Dale

Fig. 5.4. A discriminative stimulus. The bait bag (left) indicates that reinforcement is available. During competition, with the bait bag gone (right), the dog may abandon previously learned behaviors.

failing score as dogs who fail to retrieve at all. Because dogs are not as ver-
bally oriented as we are, it is important that you teach your dog the significance of the cue. The best way to do that is to teach the dog that the presence
of the cue indicates that he might be reinforced.

Anticipation is another indication of the influence of discriminative
stimuli. Dogs prefer to take their cues from the environment rather than from
the spoken word. If other environmental signs are present that indicate the
availability of appetitives or aversives, they may not need the handler's verbal
cue because the other environmental signals tell them reinforcement is available. Anticipation occurs when the dog offers the behavior before he has been
given the cue. But from his point of view, other factors in the environment
have already provided the cue. He is still responding to a stimulus; it's just the
wrong one.

One of the most anticipated of all obedience exercises occurs in the
Open class. Dogs new to the Open exercises most often anticipate the drop in
the *Drop on Recall* exercise. When I began to exhibit my first obedience dog
in the Open class, I found that most judges would signal me to drop him
opposite the high jump. (I think this was because it gave the judges a visual
point whereby they could measure the promptness of the dog's response to the
command.) Soon my dog would drop by the high jump all by himself prior to
my giving the command. In those days, obedience jumps were heavy, and I
was a lazy trainer and did not set up the jumps at each practice session. If the
jump was not present, the dog would always wait for my command to drop. It
was only in the ring, in the presence of the jump that this anticipation occurred. What had happened was that my dog had come to use the environment
of the obedience ring and the presence of the judge and high jump as predictors for the drop. In effect, the presence of the judge, his command, "Call your
dog," and the physical presence of the jump told the dog when and where to
drop. The environment replaced the command.

A knowledgeable trainer should guard against the emergence of discriminative stimuli as command-givers and should carefully establish the
verbal cue as the only discriminative stimulus. Unless this is explicitly done,
other elements in the environment may furnish the relevant information to the
dog who will not wait to be told to perform the exercise. It is far easier for
most dogs to respond to environmental or body cues than it is for them to

learn to wait for verbal ones. You can take advantage of this by substituting, as often as possible, signals and body motions for words.

A friend of mine, Lois, had a terrible time training her Keeshond to perform the obedience *Recall* exercise correctly. Misty would almost always come to Lois before she was called, and we couldn't figure out why this was happening. Finally, after we stopped looking at the dog and watched the handler, we saw the reason. Lois had unconsciously adopted a very methodical approach to the recall. As she left Misty, she looked at the ground and continued to do so until she turned to face the dog. (Lois did this to make sure she was walking a straight line and to ensure that her feet were lined up before she called the dog). Right before she called Misty, Lois would transfer her gaze from the ground to the dog. As soon as eye contact was established, Misty would get up and come in. The dog had come to associate the eye contact with the command to come, much the same way that Amber had associated the hiking boots with a walk in the woods. Lois's eye contact, in effect, became Misty's command to come.

Once we identified the problem, it was easy to fix. Misty did many stays with Lois making eye contact and recalls without eye contact (Fig. 5.5). Once we made it clear to Misty that she would only be reinforced if she responded to the correct stimulus, the anticipation disappeared. In this case, as in many cases of anticipation, it was not that the behavior hadn't been trained, it was that the exact cue for the behavior had not been clarified.

The Trainer as the Focus of Attention

Once the trainer has employed the strategy of making the training area as similar to the ring environment as possible (thus reducing the chance of the dog being distracted by new elements in his environment) and trained the dog to respond to the appropriate elements (cues) in that environment, it's time to employ the second strategy: teach the dog how to focus. No one can exactly duplicate all aspects of a performance environment. Dress rehearsal is radically different from the first night's performance. Therefore, the trainer needs to find a way to focus the dog's attention on the task in such a way that the environment does not interfere.

Attention is the key. Although many people teach attention as a means to good heeling, attention has another invaluable function. Just as it serves to focus the dog on the trainer, it also helps the dog to ignore new and potentially

Victoria A. Dale

Fig. 5.5. Misty's problem was fixed by practicing stays with the handler making eye contact (left), and recalls without eye contact (right).

threatening additions to his environment (Fig. 5.6). You remember the old-fashioned movie scene — the heroine is stranded on a very high place and she is terrified. Her rescuer says, "Don't look down, don't look down. Just look into my eyes and do what I tell you." Our heroine does as she is told and all ends happily. The movie scene shares a common principle with dog training. If the dog is focusing on his person, his performance won't be disrupted by a distracting environment.

But take care. As adept as they are at reading the environment, our dogs are even better at reading us. What we do, what we say, how we dress, and how we stand or walk are all sources of information that our dogs understand. If we consistently train in old blue jeans, turn our heads to look at the dog when we heel, talk happily to him during and between exercises, and then dress up for the ring, look forward and never talk to the dog, chances are he is going to think something is wrong. A well-trained dog regards his trainer as his most significant source of environmental information. The trainer must take care not to alter those signals in such a way that the dog either doesn't recognize them or perceives them as threatening.

Fig. 5.6. The trainer must find a way to focus the dog's attention on the task so that the environment does not interfere.

Good trainers capitalize on their dogs' environmental sensitivity and use their physical posture, facial expressions, and tone of voice to reassure and convey as much information as possible to the dog. For example, consider the environments of two Novice obedience exercises, the *Long Sit* and the *Recall*. In both exercises, there are similar environmental conditions — the dog is placed in a sit position and the handler crosses to the other side of the ring. Yet these exercises require two very different behaviors from the dog. On a stay, he must remain in place until the handler has returned to him, whereas on a recall, he must get up and come in to the handler. Until the dog understands the differences between these two exercises, he is liable to mistake one for the other. Inexperienced dogs often fidget uneasily on a stay for several seconds and then get up and reluctantly walk in to the handler. Their whole physical posture indicates uncertainty. They seem to say, "I think I'm supposed to come to you, but I'm really not sure."

Good trainers creates differences in the environment to help the dog understand the appropriate behaviors. Since stays are always done with several dogs sitting next to each other in row, most trainers refuse to call their dogs out of similar lines in training situations. They want the dog to use the presence of the other dogs as an environmental cue for them to maintain their position. And although the trainer stands at the same distance across the ring as in a recall, the smart one alters her physical posture for the two exercises. On a recall, she will stand erect, weight evenly distributed on both feet, arms hanging naturally at her sides. On a stay, there is no such requirement so she folds her arms or puts them behind her back (Fig. 5.7). She might also place more weight on one foot than the other and position her feet slightly apart with one knee bent. She is trying to present an entirely different picture to the dog that is required to stay than she does when he is expected to come. Dogs are far less likely to confuse a stay with a recall when there are significant environmental dissimilarities.

Food as a Source of Information

It should come as no surprise, therefore, that the presence or absence of food or toys in the environment is a potent source of information about the availability of reinforcement. Dogs that are heavily food trained use all sorts of predictors as information about reinforcement. The bait bag, the physical

Fig. 5.7. The trainer may use body position to help the dog discriminate between the Novice *Stay* exercise and the *Recall*.

presence of food on the trainer's person, and even the presence of food in the training ring signals to the dog that food is available. If the dog is weaned off primary reinforcement or the presence of primary reinforcements (like food) too abruptly, he seems to go on strike. "No food, no work!" he seems to say. Although trainers often attribute this kind of behavior to a conscious choice of the dog and say, "He knows you can't feed him in the ring so he is disobeying you," it may simply be that the dog is responding automatically to the absence of something that told him reinforcement was possible.

Although trainers often try to fool their dogs by reinforcing them with food at matches, eventually a campaigned dog will learn the difference. He will come to associate the ring environment with the unavailability of primary reinforcement like food or toys. The atmosphere at a match is quite different from that of a show; the ring boundaries, judges, and audience at a show (as well as the trainer's own attitude) are not the same. And a show is very different indeed from the familiar confines of the dog's usual training site.

Dogs that are not weaned off dependence on food in training soon come to see the ring environment as a predictor that food will not be forthcoming. In these cases, when the availability of reinforcement disappears, so do the behaviors. Good trainers use as many ways as they can to help their dogs get used to performing in environments in which some of the signals have been changed. In addition to making the training environment similar to that of the ring and to teaching the dog to focus on only the trainer, they establish strong conditioned reinforcers that can be used inside the ring. They also seek to acclimate the dog to working for longer and longer periods of time without reinforcement. All of these strategies help the dog make the transition from training to performance.

Doing Without Food

During competition, a dog must offer performances repeatedly, often several times a day without any external primary reinforcement. Therefore, it's essential that you teach your dog to do without food or toys at least for a finite period of time. He must become accustomed to doing an entire performance without external reinforcement before formal exposure to competition. This is important to prevent your dog from forming an association between competition and lack of reinforcement. The dog should be weaned gradually from reinforcement during its training career, rather than all at once.

The following is a typical schedule for weaning from primary rein-forcement. Once your dog is able to offer a consistent behavior on a variable schedule of (fixed or ratio, depending on the exercise), begin to introduce brief training sessions (perhaps consisting of only one exercise) in which only conditioned reinforcement is available. If you are training in your front yard, give your dog a treat only after you leave the area and go into the house. If you are working at a park or school yard, leave the treats in the car and reward the dog only at the end of the training session. If your dog's behavior deterio-rates, terminate the session rather than reverting to food, or you'll teach the dog that if he holds out long enough, the food will come out again. As the performance of each exercise improves, you can begin to ask your dog to perform more than one exercise at a time without reinforcement. With a Novice obedience dog, you might ask for *On-Leash Heeling* followed by the *Stand for Exam* exercise with no reinforcement. Do this first at home, then in another environment. You might then ask for *On-Leash Heeling*, the *Stand for Exam* and *Off-Leash Heeling* in much the same fashion. Work toward the goal of having your dog perform the whole Novice routine without food, toys, or games, both in a familiar environment and in a new one, before asking him to do that at a trial.

This does not mean that the dog will never be offered food or another primary reinforcer again in a training situation. It just means that occasionally reinforcement will not be available. The dog must learn to be willing to work when external reinforcement is not available, just as he must be willing to work in the rain and in the hot sun, under conditions that are less than perfect.

Your approach to matches should be similar. Although your dog's initial exposures to the more formal performance venue should include lots of food both inside and outside the ring, your final goal is a complete perfor-mance without food. Gradually remove the food from the ring. First, put it on the judge's table, then on a chair outside the ring (Fig. 5.8), and finally leave it in your car. Reinforce the performance of an individual exercise by running with the dog to the location of the treat. You should gradually ask for more and more behaviors without reinforcement as the dog gains experience. As with your training sessions, don't remove food from the match ring all at one time, and never take the food away permanently. Even after you have a satis-factory run without any reinforcement, you may feed in the ring at various times — if you are having trouble with an exercise, if your dog seems to lack confidence, or just for the sheer unexpected impact of a sudden jackpot.

Not All Reinforcement is Good

Even though food and toys are valuable tools for information and motivation, there are times when they can actually be detrimental to a dog's willingness to perform. If the entire focus of the dog is devoted to obtaining the external motivator, if the only reason for performance is that piece of food or that squeaky toy, then you may be neglecting a key element in your dog's performance — that of making the activities themselves and of working with you reinforcing. This is necessary for long-term success in competition.

A Personal Example

I once took a course in theories of learning because I was interested in exploring the science of operant conditioning. Most of the course was devoted to the theory of operant conditioning, and one of the assignments was for each student to design an experiment in which they improved an aspect of their behavior using operant conditioning. Although most students chose things like exercising more or eating more healthy food, I chose to increase my daily water intake since this was something I could measure even at work. My goal was to expand my consumption to the eight glasses per day recommended by some physicians. I designed my experiment well, with gradually increasing demands per day and with incentives for goals met on a daily, weekly, and monthly basis. (I paid myself by depositing money into an account which could only be spent on a fun activity.) At the end of the six week experiment, I was drinking eight glasses of water a day and had earned enough money to go to a dog seminar, stay at a nice motel, and eat really good food.

Victoria A. Dale

Fig. 5.8. Your goal is performance without. Gradually remove the food from the ring to a chair outside it (left), then to the car. During the transition period, run with your dog to the treats for a reward (right).

But the day after the experiment ended, and reinforcement for drinking the water was no longer available, my water intake reverted immediately to what it had been before. There was no gradual tailing off, no slow slide to my previous levels — it was an immediate free fall. No reinforcement, no eight glasses a day. Boom! I had obviously not achieved my goal if what I wanted was a permanent change in behavior, and it was not feasible for me to spend the rest of my life paying myself for each glass of water that I drank.

The pitfall of my experiment, and the pitfall of much of operant conditioning, was that I had not made any attempt to make water drinking intrinsically reinforcing. I drank only because there was going to be a payoff at the end of the day. The same thing happens to many dogs that are trained only with external reinforcements like games, food, and toys. These dogs may do well in the beginning levels of competition, especially if they are shown sparingly, and thus still believe that there will be food for their performances. However, by the time they get to the more advanced levels where the performance is more difficult and they are in the ring for longer periods, their performance begins to deteriorate.

Bottom Line:
Behaviors based only on external reward systems — systems that do not appeal to the animal intrinsically — do not hold up over time, even on a variable schedule of reinforcement.

Confirmation From Wall Street

There is confirmation from the business world on precisely this point. Alfie Kohn, in an article entitled "*Why Incentive Plans Cannot Work*" says, "Do rewards work? The answer depends on what we mean by work. Research suggests that by-and-large, rewards succeed at securing one thing only: temporary compliance. When it comes to producing lasting change in attitudes and behaviors, rewards, like punishment, are strikingly ineffective. Once the rewards run out, people revert to their old behaviors."[1] In fact, Kohn argues, not only are rewards ineffective in producing long-term behavior changes, they often leave the subject less likely to offer the desired behaviors.

Why is this? Here are the reasons Kohn gives. First, rewards can punish. If we have been taught to expect a reward, suddenly not receiving it is

---

[1]A. Kohn.*Why Incentive Plans Cannot Work*, Harvard Business Review, Sept.-Oct. 1993, pp. 55-56.

indistinguishable from being punished. The more desirable the reward is, the more demoralizing it is to miss out on it. Second — and this is of primary importance for the dog trainer — rewards rupture the relationship between the rewarder and the one who is rewarded. They seem to interfere with the establishment of loyalty between the pair. In dog training, rewards tend to focus the attention of the dog away from the trainer and toward what is being offered. Third, rewards undermine interest. Few will be shocked to learn that extrinsic motivation is a poor substitute for genuine interest in one's performance. What is far more surprising is that rewards, like punishment, may actually interfere with the intrinsic motivation that is needed for optimal performance.

Food, toys, and games still play an important role in training. But most experienced trainers, those who have trained many dogs to perform repeatedly in competition events, believe that positive and negative reinforcement (external reinforcement) are not the only keys to maximizing the dog's performance. Trainers also need to work hard to ensure that the training relationship, that connection between human and dog that makes the team work well together, has been firmly established before the team steps into the ring. This is not an easy task, especially when it seems so easy to get the puppy to work for just a tiny piece of hot dog. But this relationship, once established, will stand a trainer in far better stead than all the food in the world.

Teaching for Relationships

Think how neatly this dovetails with the need for the dog to focus on the trainer as a strategy for overcoming environmental fears! Focus and relationship can be mutually reinforcing. The more focused the dog is on the trainer, the better the relationship, and the stronger the relationship, the easier it will be for the trainer to ask the dog for total focus. The creation of this kind of relationship is something that should begin well before the team ever considers competition. The foundations that you lay in your training sessions will support deeper trust and reliance as you and your dog advance to the more sophisticated levels of your sport.

As a trainer, you should spend a lot of training time making yourself interesting to your dog, even as you move about between exercises. Play little informal games (Fig. 5.9). Teach the dog to bounce at your side and touch your finger with his nose as you go from one exercise to the next. If you can establish these games, training will be interesting and fun for your dog. The games will be something to look forward to after the successful completion of an exercise, and your presence will be more reinforcing to the dog than anything else. And although you may not be able to take cookies into the ring, you certainly can take yourself!

Fig. 5.9. Spend time making yoursel interesting to your dog. Play games that stimulate him.

Chapter 6. What Pavlov Knew

Principle:
CLASSICAL CONDITIONING

The Story of Alex

One Friday night in 1995 I joined several other Border Collie owners for a judges' seminar. Several conformation judges, in town for a local show, had asked to see Border Collies. They wanted to examine several different examples of the breed before Border Collies became eligible to be shown in conformation classes. We set up a ring outdoors at their motel and proudly asked our dogs to strut their stuff. Six handlers brought about 18 dogs with obedience titles ranging from CD to OTCh. It was shady in the ring and we were having a good time relaxing and talking dogs. The dogs not being shown were tied to stakes outside the ring waiting their turn. They were all well-trained and trustworthy, we were close by, and none of us was worried about their safety.

Suddenly I caught a movement out of the corner of my eye. Carol's dog, Alex, had pulled her leash from the stake and was slowly, step by step, inching away from the ring. Alex, 7 years old, was a stable dog, trained by a person who had extended formal obedience to the home environment. Alex had impeccable manners; she would not dream of being disobedient. Nothing unusual had happened — there had been no loud noises, nothing to spook a dog — and Alex had always been a steady dog. Her behavior was totally uncharacteristic.

I called to Carol, who handed the dog she was holding to a friend, and slowly stepped over the baby gates toward Alex. She softly commanded Alex to lie down, but Alex ignored her, just as she subsequently ignored a thrown dumbbell and Carol's command to retrieve (and Alex is a fanatic retriever). Although Alex didn't bolt, she kept inching further and further away from the ring. It was as though she wanted to come to Carol but couldn't. Carol didn't try to approach Alex directly but took an oblique route, because Alex was moving slowly but inexorably toward a four-lane highway that was hidden from the ring by a fringe of pine trees but only twenty yards away. It was rush hour, and we could scarcely hear Carol's soft commands to her dog over the traffic. Everything seemed to be happening in slow motion.

There was nothing any of us could do; we took tighter holds on our own dogs' leads, and Carol's friend Betsy knelt beside Carol's other dogs and hugged them to her. We couldn't see the road from where we were. We didn't want to. Carol and Alex disappeared through the trees, and we withdrew into ourselves, prepared for the screech of brakes, the thud, the yelp, and the cries of one friend who had just lost another.

By the grace of God, *nothing* happened! Carol and Alex made it across that four-lane highway. Cars pulled over to the side, compassionate drivers jammed on brakes and gave the woman and dog space to pass slowly and safely across the road. Somewhere on the other side, Alex regained enough composure to allow Carol to come to her and pick up the leash. The seminar progressed, and we all acted normally. But later that night, shock set in, and I replayed the incident over and over in my mind. Why did Alex do that? Why would such a well-trained dog, in the absence of anything we could see, ignore the commands of the person she had obeyed without hesitation every day of her life?

History

When Alex was a young dog she had developed a severe stay problem. It originated from a reaction she had to some sudden loud barking ringside just as Carol left her on the obedience *Sit-Stay* exercise. Although she made it through Novice obedience because she was kept in position by Carol's presence in the ring, she was clearly frightened at being left alone in a line of dogs. The out-of-sight stays of Open obedience were too much for her to handle. Carol repeatedly returned from the required three minute absence to find Alex curled in a tight ball, head turned away from the ring. Although Carol is an excellent trainer and worked hard to fix the problem, Alex would not hold the sit and could not progress to Utility even though she knew the exercises to perfection. At last we hit upon a solution, one that had worked with another dog with a similar problem. Alex was corrected for lying down on the sit by having her handler splash a cup of water in her face. Although this was not painful, the suddenness of the drenching produced the desired effect. Not only did Alex hold her stays in the three shows for her CDX, Carol had to physically force her out of the sit to do the *Long Down* exercise.

Carol thought that the problem had been permanently solved until she took Alex to Canada to get her Canadian CDX. Suddenly the problem re-emerged, but in a much more severe fashion. The first time Carol came into view upon returning to the ring, Alex broke and ran from the ring. She did it again at the second trial, and Carol decided it would be pointless to continue to show her. The problem worsened, and Alex broke stays in training session after training session. The only thing Carol could think of that might have triggered this behavior was that there had been a cup of water on the judge's table at the Canadian show. We hypothesized that the cup had suddenly re-minded Alex of the thrown water, and that she then associated the punishment with the returning handler. It broke Carol's heart to see the dog she loved so much run away from her.

Carol worked to solve this problem for a year. She totally retrained Alex's stays using only positives. Alex was reinforced as Carol came into sight, she was released toward Carol who threw a ball for her, and slowly, she began to tolerate Carol's return. (None of this affected Alex's enthusiasm for obedience. She worked happily in all other exercises and scored high enough to qualify for the Regional Superdog Class.) When Alex stopped exhibiting signs of stress at Carol's return, she was entered in the Open classes at UKC obedience trials and breezed right through, stays and all.

And then came that Friday at the motel. Later we replayed the events in our minds and decided to try an experiment in safer conditions the next week. Carol sat on a lawn chair with Alex sitting at her left. On the ground to Carol's right was a white plastic cup. Carol reached down with her right hand, picked up the cup and upended it. She moved slowly and quietly, said nothing to Alex and made no eye contact with her. But as soon as Carol touched the cup, Alex sprang to the end of her leash — ears back, eyes rolling in fear.

This is what we now believe happened that Friday when Alex ran away. When Carol returned to the group of dogs, she had tossed a collar down beside Alex as she lay outside the ring. This triggered Alex's memory of the tossed cup of water. Even though Alex understood that she should not leave, and every ounce of her operant conditioning-based training told her she must obey, the fear of that cup of water overrode all her previous training. Alex was, in effect, forced to disobey; her behavior was governed not by operant, but by **classical conditioning.**

Alex had not forgotten how to be obedient, but her fear overpowered her ability to hold the stay and then to come when Carol called her. Her performance training, based on operant conditioning, did not take into account the dog's emotional state. All of the retraining that Carol had done did not address the real problem. Alex had long understood the command, "Stay." It was her fear, first of loud and sudden barking, and later of the cup of water, that made it impossible for her to obey. Our ignorance of the true cause of the problem almost caused great harm where obedience really matters, when obeying a command is a matter of life or death. Neither of us had any idea that Alex could or would generalize her experience and feel fear when an object such as a collar was thrown to the ground beside her.

Emotion and Learning

One of the lessons that Alex's story teaches is that learning and per-forming do not occur in a vacuum. Dogs respond emotionally to many things in the course of training and performing. In particular, the dog's emotional response to the environment plays a major role in his ability to offer even the best learned behaviors. When we train our dogs, we are not writing upon blank slates. All of our activities occur in environments that have the potential not only to furnish information to the dogs, but to imprint strong emotional associations upon them. Behaviorists train rats and pigeons in laboratory boxes and thus control environmental variables and minimize their emotional effects. Dog trainers, however, have no such boxes and must pay close atten-tion to the effects such variables have on dogs' learning processes.

The effects of emotion on behavior are pervasive and powerful. Few animals, canine or human, are immune to them. The relationship between emotions and behavior is the realm of classical conditioning, which deals with the role of the environment in the formation of emotional associations, the power of emotion, and the process of association itself. It is a powerful theory which has been vastly under-used by dog trainers. Unless a training program pays as much attention to the dog's emotional state as it does to his cognitive one, well-learned behaviors may never have the chance to fully emerge.

A Brief History of Classical Conditioning

Classical conditioning, also called Pavlovian conditioning after the discoveries of Russian psychologist Ivan Pavlov, predates operant conditioning. In addition to dealing with the effects of emotion on behavior, it also explores the concept of association, without which the science of operant conditioning would be impossible. Remember that the effectiveness of operant conditioning is dependent upon an animal's ability to associate reinforcement with a particular behavior and thus choose to offer it again. It is this ability to pair stimulus and response that makes learning possible.

Unlike operant conditioning, classical conditioning does not deal directly with voluntary animal behavior. Classical conditioning deals with the emotional associations that strongly affect voluntary behaviors. The primary importance of classical conditioning to the dog trainer is that it explains how environmental stimuli affect both our own and our dogs' emotional reactions and how those emotional reactions, in turn, affect behaviors.

Terminology

At this point, it is useful to define some technical terms that will be important later in the discussion. Pavlov observed that offering meat powder to dogs caused them to salivate. He also observed that if the meat powder was systematically offered by lab workers at a given time, the dogs would begin to salivate at the sight of the workers arriving at feeding time. To explore this, Pavlov started ringing a bell immediately prior to the delivery of the meat to the dogs. In the beginning, the sound of the bell had no effect upon the dogs. But after it was paired with the delivery of food, the dogs would salivate at its sound regardless of whether meat was present or not. The dogs had come to associate the bell with food, and this caused them to salivate.

One of the main differences between classical and operant conditioning is the type of behaviors they explain. Classical conditioning is concerned with reflexive responses — behaviors, like salivation, that are not under voluntary control. Although beyond an animal's control, such reflexive behaviors are indicative of the emotional state of an animal, and that emotional state, in turn, strongly affects the dog's ability to offer voluntary behaviors.

Pavlov termed the meat the **unconditioned stimulus** and defined salivation as an **unconditioned response**. They are unconditioned because the dogs did not have to *learn* to salivate at the sight of meat — it occurred naturally. When Pavlov paired the ringing of the bell with the delivery of the meat, the bell became a **conditioned stimulus** for salivation. The bell was termed conditioned because the dog associated its sound with being fed. The dog was conditioned to salivate at the sound of the bell. The salivation caused by the ringing of the bell was termed a **conditioned reflex**; Pavlov called it **conditioned** because it was the result of a conditioned stimulus (the bell) as opposed to a natural one (presentation of food).

The ringing of the bell provided information to the dog about the availability of reinforcement. It gave him information about what resources were available to him in the environment. If environmental stimuli are aversive, they cause defensive conditioned responses; if they are pleasurable, they cause appetitive conditioned responses. We have already seen how important environmental clues are to animals as sources of information about the friendliness or hostility of the environment. In particular, these stimuli are the main predictors of the availability of reinforcement. But in addition, the nature of the information presented (aversive or appetitive) also contributes to the formation of an emotional response on the part of the animal.

Conditioned Emotional Responses

If the environment is associated with the unavailability of resources or with aversive stimuli, the environment creates a response of fear or anxiety in the animal. This effect is termed **conditioned fear.** Let me give you two examples, one from my training experience and the other from the laboratory.

When Tiger was a young dog, he developed a pillow fetish. If I left without moving all of my pillows from his reach, I would return to find the living room strewn with feathers (Fig. 6.1). I knew I couldn't punish Tiger for his transgression since there was a long gap of time between his indulgence and my return, but I was put in a bad mood by the necessity of spending many minutes dislodging feathers from the furniture and from my long-coated dogs. So I crabbed and sulked and was not, in general, much fun to be around. Amber (who had nothing to do with the pillow destruction) came to see feathers as a predictor of my foul mood. She developed a fear of all feathers (Fig. 6.2). Imagine my mother's surprise when a stray feather from a pillow she had picked up sent Amber running under the bed. "Some Lassie," she chuckled when I explained, "Good thing Collies are expected to herd sheep and not pillows."

The second example comes from a laboratory experiment. Using the principles of operant conditioning, a rat was trained to press a lever for food. Once the lever-pressing behavior was well established, the conditions were changed. The lever and the food dispenser were removed from the rat's cage. Periodically a tone was sounded, followed by a brief, mild electric shock. After a period of time, the lever and the food dispenser were placed back in the cage. Although the rat resumed his lever pressing activity almost immediately, he would abandon it at the sound of the tone, even when the tone was no longer followed by the shock.

The experimenters reasoned that the tone suppressed the lever pressing behavior. They labeled the abandonment of lever pressing activity a **conditioned emotional response**. In this case, it was conditioned suppression. In more anthropomorphic terms, they concluded that the tone associated with the shock produced fear in the rat. As the rat became fearful, he lost interest in food, and hence stopped offering behaviors to obtain food since the food was no longer perceived as reinforcing.

Fig. 6.1. An example of a conditioned emotional response. Tiger plays with a pillow while Amber watches and worries.

131

Fig. 6.2. As a consequence of Tiger's misbehavior with pillows, Amber developed a fear of feathers.

Remember that classical conditioning deals only with involuntary or reflexive behaviors such as emotional responses. The rat had no control over whether he became frightened or not. The rat's fear caused him to abandon his lever-pressing activity which was voluntary. Thus, the involuntary response affected a voluntary one. Similarly, Amber's fear of feathers (involuntary response) made her flee (a voluntary behavior).

Applications to Dog Training

As dog trainers, we must take great care to be aware of the effects of the environment upon our carefully trained dogs. If we inadvertently create a situation in which the dog develops a negative emotional association with the environment, the dog may become incapable of offering trained behaviors. A person suffering from severe claustrophobia may be incapable of answering questions correctly on a test if the testing site is a small enclosed room, even if he is perfectly capable of answering correctly outside the room. Likewise, a highly trained agility dog who has learned to be afraid of thunder may be unable to run a simple course if he hears the rumble of an approaching storm.

Chapter 4 discussed the phenomenon of discriminative stimuli. Dogs that have been trained only in their owners' backyards or at a familiar training building often cease to offer trained behaviors when asked to perform in a new environment. Marine mammal trainers call it New Tank Syndrome because it explains why learned behaviors of marine mammals degenerate when they are placed in a different tank to perform. Like our dogs, these animals use familiar environments as predictors of reward. They are secure. But the new environment is devoid of that information. They become uncertain because many of the environmental cues that they have come to associate with pleasure and safety are absent. They become distracted and cannot concentrate on their trainers because they are reacting emotionally to their new circumstances.

Rather than understanding that this distraction is a normal response to a new environment, the trainer may correct for lack of attention because she is convinced that the dog really does understand what is expected and is choosing to be disobedient. If this happens often enough, the trainer makes the dog's first exposures to new environments very negative. And so a negative association begins to form, and with it the beginnings of a fearful response to all new situations. Once the dog is afraid, he may be unable to offer correct behaviors. Although the trainer may intend her corrections to be associated with the dog's behavior, the dog may associate those aversives with the newness of the environment and become unable to perform in all new environments.

If this pattern continues, the dog will come to regard an environmental change as a conditioned stimulus — a stimulus that he has been conditioned to believe predicts an aversive experience. He will develop a conditioned negative emotional response to going to new places. If there are similar objects, events, and happenings in the various new environments (jumps, baby gates, judges, spectators), these become even stronger conditioned stimuli and intensify his fear. Eventually the fear of new environments which the dog has come to associate with the administration of corrections will suppress behaviors the dog was perfectly capable of offering in familiar environments.

Not only does the fear itself suppress behavior, it interferes with the appeal of appetitive stimuli to the dog. A fearful dog will no longer eat because fear suppresses appetite. Since the food is no longer reinforcing, he will not work for food reinforcements. The same is true for any stimulus that the dog previously found reinforcing (toys, play, the opportunity to work with the owner, or the exciting nature of the exercises themselves). None of these will be effective in the presence of fear.

This is why the fear continues even when the trainer ceases to correct the dog and moves to a more positive training strategy. Once a dog has come to fear the environment, or something in it, reversal of that attitude is almost impossible if the trainer tries to resolve the problem using operant conditioning. A fearful dog is neither hungry nor playful and, therefore, food and toys are no longer positively reinforcing. Praise and petting and trainer attention are often not enough either. Negative reinforcement and punishment are ineffective too. Dogs frequently shut down when they are frightened and become unable to offer any behaviors at all, even if they are punished. The dog's attention is far more focused on escaping the situation than it is on obtaining treats or avoiding corrections. The dog does not respond to the trainer's commands because he is no longer aware of them.

Generalization

Dogs often generalize from the environment, and this ability can get a dog and trainer in big trouble. Dogs that are initially frightened by thunder can easily generalize that fear to other loud noises. Firecrackers, gunshots, even the banging of port-a-potty doors at dog shows can render a dog incapable of performing. Such generalized fears not only affect performance but other activities, too. I have three dogs who are afraid of thunder. It is pointless for me to feed them during a storm because they are no longer hungry. Commands to get off issued to a frightened dog who is trying to climb into my lap might as well not be given. Punishing a dog for fear-based behaviors only makes the dog more frightened of the original and the generalized stimuli. Frightened dogs are not willful, disobedient creatures; they are temporarily disconnected from their ability to offer trained behaviors. When the fear passes, so will this inability.

Alex generalized from a thrown cup of water to a tossed collar. The fear that the generalization caused made her unable to obey her trainer. Alex had not forgotten to come or to retrieve. She had not ceased to love Carol or to want to please her. But that fear suppressed her obedience behaviors. Fear made her want to flee the situation, and her desire to get away from what she perceived as a hostile environment made her incapable of being reinforced by the safety of her handler's presence and the desire for her handler's approval.

Ringwise

It is not uncommon for a dog's behavior to degenerate in a competition situation. Dogs that work wonderfully in practice and even in matches often seem to suffer inexplicable memory losses once they go to a real show. A common response from trainers is to say that their dogs are ringwise. Most trainers would agree that this wrongly assigns vindictive emotional motivations to dogs. Explanations that suggest that the dog is using the ring to gain canine revenge or that postulate that the dog is disobeying because he knows he can't be corrected are needlessly far fetched. Classical conditioning offers a much simpler explanation.

Radical changes in canine behavior often indicate that something in the environment is distracting the dog. One of two things must be true. The environment may be intrinsically so threatening that the dog needs to pay more attention to it than the trainer. A dog that breaks a stay at the sound of thunder is a good example. Alternately, the trainer may have inadvertently taught the dog that the competition environment is a perilous one, and the dog thus refuses to obey commands. In both cases, the reflexive response is fear, and it is fear that prevents the dog from complying with the commands.

The Education of a Ringwise Dog

I am often asked to judge obedience matches and in the past have usually accepted these invitations. I believe that we are obligated to give something back to our respective sports, and an easy way to do this is to help out if we are asked. But over the years I have come to dread the request because I see far too many trainers using the match environment in a way that sabotages their training efforts and their relationships with their dogs. Although these trainers do not intend to cause fear or anxiety, by constantly correcting their dogs in the ring, they create an association between the corrections and the ring environment that is very difficult to erase.

One summer I judged a Novice class for my club's obedience fun match. I try to concentrate exclusively on the team that is performing in the ring, but this day my attention kept being drawn to a woman with a Wire-Haired Fox Terrier standing just outside my ring. She warmed the dog up for so long that each time I called a new team into the ring, I was sure they would be next. As I judged the first group of stays, I watched them outside the ring. It was a warm day and although the little dog was clearly getting more and more uncomfortable in the sun, he still had a typical terrier's interest in his surroundings, especially in all the dogs that were nearby. He was very curious about all the activity around him. Each time he looked around, the woman jerked his collar and commanded, "Watch me." Although the dog seemed bright and attentive when I first saw him, by the time his trainer brought him into to the ring, he was hot and worried; his ears were back, his tail down, and he panted heavily.

The trainer heeled him over to the starting point, giving him a few collar pops on the way. She appeared to be nervous and a little angry, too. She had great trouble getting her dog to line up to begin the heeling exercise. He would sit crooked and she would heel him in a circle. He would look away, and she would pop him. This caused him to sit even more crookedly, and she would begin the process all over again. Her attitude and behavior were deteriorating as rapidly as the dog's. Finally she looked at me in exasperation and said, "He never acts like this in practice. He knows how to heel."

I tried to put her at ease and to distract her from her constant corrections by asking her if this was the dog's first match. "No," she told me. They had been to many matches, and the dog had been getting progressively worse. I suggested that she try to use some sort of motivator, food or a toy, to help the dog with his performance. "Oh no," she said in horror, "I don't want him to think he can be fed in the ring. He needs to learn he can't get away with being a bad dog here."

The *Heel on Lead* exercise was a disaster. The dog was very distracted by my presence and appeared to be confused by the trainer's increasingly exasperated commands and rigid posture. The poor fellow was corrected on almost every step of the heeling pattern. Before we began the *Figure Eight* exercise I again asked the trainer if she would like to try to help the dog do the pattern. She replied that the dog "had to learn to do it right in the ring by himself." He was a defiant dog, she said, and she didn't want him to think that he could get away with misbehavior in the ring. As soon as she removed his leash for the *Stand for Exam* exercise, he ran out of the ring (Fig. 6.3). As the handler left in pursuit, she looked back over her shoulder at me and said, "See, he's ringwise already!"

This trainer chose to interpret her dog's behaviors as willful disobedience, as an attempt to "get away with something." Her reasoning was that the dog had somehow come to believe that, if he was in the ring, he couldn't be corrected for being wrong, and so he had decided not to obey the commands. This is what she meant by ringwise — that the dog was in control of the situation and was somehow using the AKC Obedience Rule Book to defy her.

Fig. 6.3. Once the handler entered the ring, she behaved very differently, and the dog was very confused and ran away.

It was clear to me that this was not even remotely true. The dog was not wise to the ring — he was terrified of it. He had come to associate the obedience ring with corrections and other negative experiences ranging from lack of positive reinforcement to his trainer's verbal and physical displeasure. He had no idea what he needed to do to regain control of the situation because the trainer was too angry at him to give him help. He was well on the road to learning that all matches and shows were bad places. His trainer had created this association by making every one of his match experiences unpleasant from the time he got out of his car until the time he got back to his safe house. I saw this same trainer at a match six months later. She had gotten rid of her dog, because, she said, "Terriers can't do obedience." She had a new puppy ordered — a Golden Retriever — that was sure to be a winner.

This is an extreme case of misinterpreted behavior and mistaken diagnosis. Most of us do not get rid of our cherished companions to get Golden Retrievers. And those who regard breed as the only relevant characteristic of dog training are as doomed to fail with their new breed as they were with their original choice.

All Behaviors Are Not Equal

Before you blame the breed or the dog or even your training method, you should carefully consider why the behavior occurred. Until you can isolate the proper cause of a behavior, you cannot alter it to produce a more desirable effect. It is especially important to ascertain whether you are dealing with problems created by classical conditioning or with those created by operant conditioning. You cannot solve a problem created by classical conditioning by addressing it with operant conditioning strategies or vice versa.

If my dog cannot heel because he is afraid of the thunderstorm that is raging about him, then reteaching him to heel using another method will not help him if another storm comes along. It is equally true that helping a dog overcome his fear of thunder will not make him a better heeler if he hasn't been taught to heel correctly to begin with. Canine behavior problems have many causes, and part of being a good trainer is being a good detective and searching out the clues that reveal the real culprit.

Counterconditioning — The Solution to Problems of Classical Conditioning

Although there are ways to eliminate Pavlovian conditioned responses (e.g., fear of the ring), simply removing the conditioned stimulus is not one of them. If you have a terrible fear of snakes, the removal of snakes from your environment will eliminate your fear only as long as no snakes are present. The next time you see a snake, the fear will reemerge as strong as ever. A break from the ring will not cause ringwise dogs to forget their negative associations, just as it was clear that avoiding cups of water was not a safe solution to Alex's problem. As soon as the environment that triggered the negative emotion reemerges, so will the emotional response. An alternative strategy is needed because it is impossible to totally control the environment. You must alter the dog's response to the environment.

The best solution to a problem caused by an emotional association is **counterconditioning**. In the case of the 'ringwise' dog, the nature of the dog's association with the competition environment must be changed from negative to positive. The negative stimuli must be replaced with positive ones. The ringwise dog has learned to associate the ring (baby gates, jumps, etc.) with aversive stimuli (physical corrections, handler disapproval, loss of control). New unconditioned stimuli (pleasurable ones) must be introduced that are more powerful than the previous ones — pleasurable stimuli need to displace painful ones in the dog's associations.

When alcoholics are counterconditioned, a drug is administered that induces nausea and vomiting when the person drinks alcohol. The previously pleasant associations with drinking are then replaced by unpleasant ones. If a dog has formed negative associations with the ring because of repeated corrections or lack of reinforcement, the handler needs to replace the aversive stimuli with pleasant ones such as food, games, and praise. If the dog has trouble with the exercises, he should be helped, not corrected. The goal is for the dog to learn to associate the ring with pleasant events.

Retreading Rose — A Story of Counterconditioning

Rose was a willing and very sweet Golden Retriever. Although she breezed through her beginning obedience classes and adored retrieving, she developed a fear of the high jump. She was not an athletic dog, and jumping did not come naturally to her, so she was initially hesitant to take the jump at any height at all. Her trainer, Sandy, thought that any dog ought to be able to jump at least low heights and corrected Rose for her refusals. The dog began to jump only because she feared the correction more than the jumping.

Once Rose was jumping full height, Sandy began to take her to matches. Rose tended to lack confidence, so Sandy gave her a lot of verbal reassurance in the ring. Rose became used to constant praise and treats and had begun to develop a good association with the ring. She performed the exercises of the Open obedience class well, and although she hesitated slightly before she took the high jump, Sandy decided she was ready to be entered in a trial.

At their first trial, Sandy was very nervous and her behavior changed dramatically. When she and Rose entered the ring, Sandy focused all of her attention on the judge and ignored Rose. Gone were the sweet talk, the treats, and the reassurance that Rose had come to depend on to overcome her fear of the jump. Rose was a very sensitive dog, and she associated the sudden lack of attention with the corrections she had received for her earlier refusals to take the jump. Her fear led to uncertainty, the uncertainty affected her takeoff, and she crashed into the jump.

Sandy decided that she must have entered Rose in shows too soon and put her back into training. In particular, she decided Rose needed to be taught how to jump all over again. And although Rose's jumping returned to its preshow level during practice sessions, her single unpleasant exposure to the show ring had replaced all of her earlier pleasant associations. Rose would willingly jump in Sandy's backyard and at the training center, but the presence of anything that remotely resembled a formal ring sent her scurrying for the car. Rose had generalized her fear of the jump to all aspects of the performance. Although she would approach the ring willingly and seemed attentive outside it, as soon as she entered the ring, her whole attitude changed. She was immediately transformed from an alert, ears up, eyes bright dog to a dog who looked as though she had been trained with a cattle prod. Ears plastered against her head, panting heavily, she would refuse to make eye contact with her handler. She responded only very slowly and reluctantly to commands, even when she was told to retrieve her beloved dumbbell. The whole performance was a disaster. Even the exercises Rose loved became sloppy and slow. She either anticipated commands or ignored them, and she would run out of the ring as soon as she completed the broad jump. It was hard for Sandy to be angry with her for this because as soon as the ring performance was over, Rose was magically restored to her happy and sweet self.

This is an example of the negative effect a dog's emotional reaction to the environment can have on performance. Here was a dog who, because of previous conditioning, had come to hate and fear the ring. It became Sandy's job to change Rose's negative associations into positive ones. Since this was an emotional problem and not a behavioral one, Sandy needed to approximate the ring environment as nearly as she could. She needed to go to many matches and to train with friends who were willing to help her create an obedience trial atmosphere. Once the simulated ring was in place, the object was for Rose to be showered with appetitive stimuli every time she entered the ring.

Jackpotting in Classical Conditioning

This is the strategy Sandy followed. She started with the location at which Rose began to show her first avoidance behavior — the entrance to the ring. She applied her counterconditioning procedure immediately before the first sign of stress. She took a handful of wonderful food that Rose was only given for a special treat, and walked her to the ring. As they approached the gate, and again as the judge approached with the measuring rod, she told Rose what a wonderful dog she was, stroked her, and let her eat the whole handful of food. She then took Rose out of the ring without doing any exercises at all and put the dog in her crate. Sandy did not pay any attention to Rose after leaving the ring, because she wanted her to associate the ring itself, not leaving the ring, with positive experiences. Later, Rose was taken back to the ring and jackpotted again. This continued until Rose was literally dragging her handler into the ring to get the treats, until the dog's entire attitude toward the ring entrance changed and Rose's behavior showed Sandy that she now perceived the ring as a good place.

The next step was to jackpot Rose as the judge measured her. If her attitude continued to be positive, Sandy did a couple of steps of heeling and then gave Rose a jackpot. It was essential that Sandy carefully observe Rose's behavior. She needed to be able to identify the subtlest signs that signaled the beginning of stress, such as lowered ear carriage, licking the lips, yawning, and reluctance to make eye contact, so that she could jackpot *immediately before* those signs occurred. She had to pay careful attention to her timing because, if she gave the jackpot after the stress had developed, she would be reinforcing the stress, and that would be counterproductive.

Sandy then gave jackpots periodically during the run-through. It took months before the effects became evident. Training of the exercises themselves continued on a normal routine, but Rose's counterconditioning was

Victoria A. Dale

Fig. 6.4. Sandy is ready to jackpot Rose just before the *High Jump* exercise, one that Rose found particularly stressful.

done within the ring environment. The jackpots were given to change Rose's emotional associations. They were independent of performance and specific only to environment.

Since Rose originally had negative associations with the high jump, Sandy did some counterconditioning with the jump in the training venue. At first, she gave a jackpot each time Rose was set up in front of the jump (Fig. 6.4). If Rose exhibited any avoidance behaviors, such as refusing to look at the jump, she reinforced Rose just for glancing toward the jump (Fig. 6.5).

Gradually Rose was weaned from jackpots in training and in the ring at matches. But there are always some jackpots at shows and at matches, although they are delivered at ringside rather than in the ring. Sandy must also be very careful not to use aversive stimuli in the ring because, unfortunately, once an association has been formed, it takes only one negative experience to reestablish all of the earlier fears. If it is necessary for Sandy to apply

Victoria A. Dale

Fig. 6.5. Rose receives a jackpot before performing the *High Jump* exercise (left), and she looks forward to jumping (right).

aversives, they are restricted to the familiar training area, a place where Rose is free of those negative associations.

Alex's Progress

And what about Alex? Once Carol knew that Alex's problem was a generalized emotional reaction, she decided to countercondition her. Because Carol could never be sure just what items would remind Alex of her earlier experiences, she decided to change Alex's associations with the original source of fear, the cup of water. She started by holding a paper plate and letting Alex eat special treats from it. As the dog indicated less and less fear, she made the plate look more and more like a cup, all the while feeding Alex from it.

When Alex would eat readily from the cup, Carol gradually introduced other environmental cues that were similar to the original situation. She would feed Alex from the cup while the dog sat in a line of other dogs (Fig. 6.6), then she would leave Alex and walk across the ring and return holding the cup filled with food. Although Alex exhibited avoidance behaviors as Carol approached (head lowered and turned aside), Carol talked soothingly to her, and Alex did not move. Carol did not go out of sight on a sit-stay until Alex was holding her stay confidently (head up, ears pricked, making direct eye contact with Carol as she returned).

Alex now holds her stays while Carol leaves her side and goes out of sight, and although she still exhibits avoidance behavior as Carol returns with the cup, she does not break. Carol always praises her and lets her eat special treats from the cup after she returns. Recently she took Alex to Canada again, and they came home with a CDX. Although Alex will never be totally free of her unpleasant associations, she now has pleasant ones to balance them, and they seem to be strong enough for Alex to be able to offer the trained behaviors she knows so well.

Fig. 6.6. Counterconditioning Alex. Gradually Alex was able to sit when the cup was held several feet away (top left), then while it was held up to her nose (top right), then when the cup was put on the ground (bottom left), and finally when she was left alone with the cup.

Chapter 7. Taking Your Show on the Road

The Principle:
COMPETITION

Now that you understand the principles of both classical and operant conditioning and how these principles can be applied to dog training, all that remains is to take those principles and translate them into a training program geared specifically to your dog and your goals.

Your End of the Leash

Before you design a training program for your dog, you should sit down and thoughtfully answer some questions about yourself and your attitudes toward dog training and the sport of dog obedience. No method of training, no matter how sophisticated, will be successful until you base your goals upon a realistic assessment of the resources that you and your dog bring to the training situation. And no method will produce the desired effects unless you believe in it and can use it with a clear conscience.

Write down a list of your goals. Then look honestly at that list and ask yourself whether your goals are truly attainable. Do you have, or can you obtain, the time, equipment, facilities, patience, energy, and ability to meet the goals? Can you realistically specify a time frame in which you intend to meet the goals or at least achieve measurable progress?

Achieving Your Goals

Whether you train your dog for obedience, field, agility, or just household manners, you must devise a specific training program that works for both you and your dog. A training program that does not specify any sort of observable outcome provides no indication of whether it is actually effective. Therefore, in addition to your larger goals, you should decide on a set of observable criteria to evaluate your progress. These criteria will help you identify the strengths and weaknesses of your training program so that you can adjust it when necessary. Be specific. Criteria such as having a better relationship with your dog or having a good obedience dog are of little help. Although these are perfectly acceptable general goals, they are too vague to be helpful as the criteria of a successful training program.

You may wish to have a dog that comes when he is called, obtains an American Kennel Club Companion Dog title, or wins an award in a national obedience competition. None of these specific goals is inherently more desirable than the others, but each demands a different level of commitment. More important, each of these goals is observable. You can see whether your dog comes when you call, the AKC will send you a Companion Dog certificate, and placing in national competitions earns you ribbons, prizes, and your picture in dog publications. There can be no ambiguity about whether your program has produced its goals.

After you define your training goals and your criteria, you need to consider your attitude toward the sport of your choice. How important is it for you to do well in competition? Do you want high scores or is qualifying for titles more important to you? Some people feel guilty about even asking their dogs to participate in competitions that they consider to be artificial. For example, many Border Collie owners argue that obedience and agility are below the dignity of a dog bred to do *real* work (stock dog work). In addition, some people do not think it is fair to ask a dog to perform for the enjoyment or fulfillment of the trainer. If you have any of these qualms, it is a safe bet that no formal training method will work for you and your dog. Your reservations will create too many barriers to your ability and willingness to communicate to your dog the specific behavior that is required and the consequences of either offering or not offering that behavior.

But let's say you've passed these tests. You have a realistic grasp of what you want, the courage to evaluate honestly how well you're progressing, and a sense that your goals are attainable for you and your dog. Now you need to consider what training method is best for you. Can you dispense food willingly and generously for a job well done? Do you like to play with your dog enough to convince him that you both are having a good time? Are you willing to work (and with some dogs it is indeed hard work) to ensure that your companion enjoys your training sessions? Many people who first learn about methods based primarily on positive reinforcement resent having to reinforce a dog for behaviors they feel he ought to offer freely. If you think that giving a dog a treat for obeying a command seems like bribery or that playing games with your dog is stupid, your reinforcement will be given grudgingly. Reinforcement that is not given freely and happily is at best totally meaningless to the dog and, at worst, terribly confusing.

On the other hand, will it be possible for you to withhold food for a job *not* well done? For many people, giving treats is self-reinforcing, and some people get so used to feeding the dog for everything he does that they feel guilty for not rewarding the least effort, even if they know the dog is capable of more. Those big brown eyes are powerful communicators. They seem to say, "No treat? You must not love me anymore." Food, toys, and games are training tools. Using them at inappropriate times can do as much damage to a dog's attitude and understanding as not using them at all.

The same consideration must be given to the application of aversives. Are you willing to apply aversives? If you are too squeamish, or feel too guilty to cause any discomfort at all, then your attempts to apply them will fail to clearly communicate the information your dog needs. You should be aware, however, that if you choose not to apply aversives, you have, by default, communicated to your dog that it is permissible for him to pursue whatever he finds most positively reinforcing at any given time. This can be very frustrating in the performance ring, and it will certainly increase the probability of inconsistent performances.

Are you willing and able to design a program of training that will enable your dog to do without food and toys for at least the time and effort it takes to give a full competition performance? This is an important consideration. All dogs must be weaned from external reinforcement gradually and by conscious design. The only reinforcers you can take into competition are the exercises themselves, your presence, and your voice. The dog that can move smoothly from backyard training to a polished competition performance with no program of transition is rare indeed. The transition can be harder to tailor to your individual dog than the exercises themselves.

The Training Picture

Dog training progresses in a spiral rather than in a straight line. Although most behaviors move from rudimentary to polished, they do not do so along an unbroken line or by a direct step-by-step progression. The slope of improvement is very gradual, and progression towards complete understanding often circles back upon itself as the trainer gradually adds all the environmental variables that are necessary for a polished ring performance (Fig 7.1). Each exercise forms its own particular spiral in the training sequence. The good trainer juggles different spiraling behaviors much as a circus performer juggles balls (Fig. 7.2). If this seems discouraging, remember that training, like juggling, is harder at the beginning. The experienced trainer has developed a feel for the dog's progress and does not always need to consciously think about how each exercise is progressing.

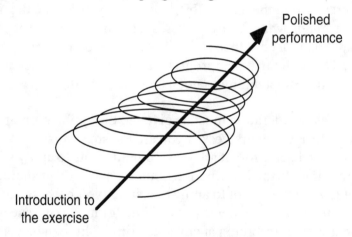

Fig. 7.1. Dogs do not learn behaviors linearly. They progress towards understanding, lose ground as new variables are introduced, and then begin to learn again as they adjust to the variables.

Anatomy of an Exercise

For the purpose of illustration, let's follow the training routine of one exercise from Open level obedience, the *Drop on Recall*, from its inception to the polished ring presentation. Remember that the introduction of the exercise is the most important training element. A dog that begins the learning process with fear or uncertainty is far more likely to revert to those emotional reactions upon experiencing difficulties later in his training than the dog whose foundations are positively presented and clearly formed.

Fig. 7.2. As a trainer, you must juggle your dog's behaviors and train at the appropriate level for each.

All training begins with the formation of step-wise goals. Although your dog need not have a clear idea of the final picture, unless you do, there will be no way to identify progress. To design a training program, you must first envision the whole exercise and then break it down into its essential components. Not only should you do your training step-by-step, you should organize the steps so that, as you put them together for the dog, he will be able to make sense of the whole exercise. To see an ideal *Drop on Recall* exercise, watch the dogs in the Open B class at an obedience trial or a national obedience competition. Even though you may not aspire to a picture-perfect drop, you will get a very clear idea of what the exercise looks like. You may choose to modify your picture to suit the physical capabilities of your dog and your own goals.

The *Drop on Recall* is one of the most difficult exercises in obedience because the dog is asked first to perform one exercise which is then interrupted before its completion by another exercise, and finally he is asked to resume the first exercise. A crude analysis yields the following parts. First is

149

the recall, where the dog must sit and stay until called, then come quickly and directly to the trainer. Second, the dog must cease his forward motion and quickly lie down. Third, he must perform another recall, coming quickly to the handler from the down position. Before training this exercise, you need to have a quick and happy recall. If your dog comes reluctantly when called, take the time to retrain that exercise now. In addition, note that the front and finish aspects of this exercise are separate elements — these should be trained and polished separately and added to the *Drop on Recall* exercise after it has been trained.

Step 1. Teaching the Drop

The first step is to teach the fold back drop where the dog drops backwards and keeps his legs under him so that he ends up crouching and ready to spring back up. Although you may have taught your dog to lie down from a stationary position, this drop is quite different. On a stay, the dog is asked to lie down from a sitting or standing position and is expected to roll over onto one hip to rest comfortably. In addition, the context is different. The dog is sitting at heel position, and handler and dog are standing in a line of other dogs and handlers. In contrast, for the moving down, the dog must drop from a different position in a different environment. The *Drop on Recall* exercise is done when the dog is moving forward towards the handler, not sitting at her side. And because the drop will be canceled almost immediately by another recall, the dog should not roll over onto a hip or get comfortable in any way. He must be ready to spring to his feet and run immediately to you on command.

Place the dog in a stand, show him a piece of food, and then lower it slowly between his front legs. As his head follows the food, move the food towards his rear (Fig. 7.3). You want the dog to fold backwards into a crouched position. This type of motion will ensure both that the dog drops from a standing position and that he drops in place without stepping forward.

If your dog doesn't know how to stand on command (and it is surprising how few novice dogs understand the 'stand' command), you should first teach it. The stand is an important foundation for the exercise, and if your dog doesn't have the proper foundations, you will likely end up retraining him at some point, because each exercise builds upon the previous ones. Once the dog understands the command to stand, you can train him to drop without

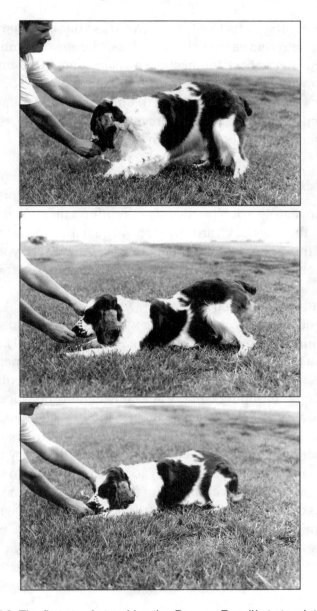

Fig. 7.3. The first step in teaching the *Drop on Recall* is to teach the fold back drop in which the dog drops backwards with his legs under him.

walking forward by using food to lure him to drop backwards as described above, or by placing a broad jump board in front of his toes to prevent forward motion.

151

When your dog starts to drop backward as your hand moves toward him, you should introduce a verbal cue such as, "Drop." The motion of your hand towards the dog's chest will become a visual signal for him to drop. Eventually, you will move the food from your hand to your mouth and then completely away from your body. You will no longer use it to lure the dog to drop, but you will still use it as a reinforcer, delivered as soon as he begins to drop at the presentation of the visual signal.

Once you have a satisfactory drop in response to your cue, you can increase your criteria for reinforcement and ask for a faster drop. You should also begin to move to a variable schedule of reinforcement. You should occasionally release the dog backwards by throwing a ball, a toy, or a piece of food behind him. At this point, you should not release him toward you since you do not want to encourage him to move forward either during or after the drop.

Adding Distance, Changing Schedules

When your dog is dropping on cue with confidence and speed, begin to increase the distance between yourself and the dog (Fig. 7.4). Although you have already put the drop on a variable schedule of reinforcement, as you begin to increase distance, you should replace that schedule with a constant one. Once the dog is dropping quickly at a considerable distance with no attempt to move forward, you can resume the variable schedule. Begin training in a familiar, secure environment, but once or twice a week try to get to another site such as a park or your club's training building. Try to get to at least one new place each week. This will accustom your dog to working in new environments and will acclimate him to traveling before he goes to work. Let the newness of the environment dictate the behaviors you will reinforce. The more unfamiliar the environment, the less complicated the behaviors and the more constant the schedule of reinforcement. Train only one small and manageable part of the drop on recall in these different environments. Other parts will follow as the dog tells you he is able to handle them.

Once the dog has advanced this far, you will need to experiment to determine which step should come next. You might want to try some informal random drops with the dog in motion but close to you (again in a familiar environment). At this point, you should only reinforce immediate responses to your command and quick drops. Any motion towards you after the command should cancel the reinforcement. If your dog indicates a lack of understanding,

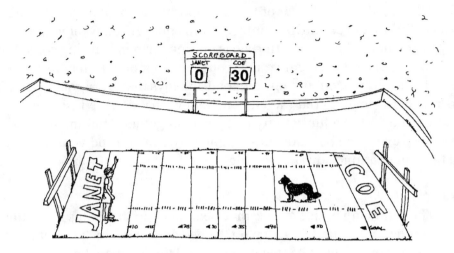

Fig. 7.4. Once your dog is dropping with confidence and speed you can introduce distance, but return to a constant schedule of reinforcement.

either by a reluctance to drop while in motion or an inability to respond to the command at a distance, try decreasing the distance between you and your dog and stepping towards the dog as you give a hand signal and a verbal cue.

Remember the spiral nature of training. When training in a new environment, prevent regression with a more constant schedule of reinforcement. The schedule of reinforcement should be governed by the dog's familiarity with both the environment and the requested behavior. Changes in either necessitate a constant schedule of reinforcement. As environment and behavior become familiar, the schedule should become more random. Always introduce a new element in a familiar environment, and wait for the dog to become confident with it before you change the schedule of reinforcement. For example, if you are training in your backyard, you might teach a new behavior (such as a drop with the dog moving towards you) using a constant schedule of reinforcement, and practice something familiar (such as a drop from behind a dowel or broad jump board) on a random schedule.

Note: Reinforcement in this context refers to both primary and secondary reinforcement. In the early stages of training, when the dog feels less confident, you should pair primary and secondary reinforcers, but as he improves in his understanding of the task, you can ask him to work sometimes just for the secondary reinforcer or for the opportunity to interact with you. Be generous with whatever kind of reinforcer you choose. You want your dog to know you are pleased with the effort he is putting forth in learning something new and a bit difficult. Remember that you want your dog ultimately to enjoy performing the drop itself, not just the food and toys that are associated with the correct performance. You want him to believe that doing a fast drop is interesting and part of a fun activity that you do together. Training for any performance event can be made into a game between you and your dog if you instill the proper attitude during training.

An Example

The following is an exercise that Bear and I do that helps make the drop fun for her. Bear likes to get up on the bed and watch me as I get ready for work. Early on, I taught her to sit, stand, and lie down on the bed as a kind of a game. As I walk around the bedroom getting dressed and putting things away, I give commands to Bear as she stands on the bed watching me. I whirl and say, "Drop," as I step toward her. If she drops quickly, I give her a quick hug; if she is slow, I push her down and then release her. My tone is happy, and I give commands and physical contact quickly and informally. Bear has played this game with me her whole life with great joy. She throws herself into the down and bounces into a stand (Fig. 7.5). The faster the better. I have incorporated signals into our little activity, and if she gets it wrong, I help. It's not a formal training session, but I ask for behaviors that are similar to ones that will eventually be required in the obedience ring. I have never once reinforced her with food or with toys for this game. It is the activity, the interaction with me, and the game itself that has become reinforcing. This is an example of working to make something intrinsically reinforcing. It's a game that is fun for both of us.

Step 2. The Drop in Motion

Combining the drop with the recall is the most difficult part of the *Drop on Recall* exercise. In the past, your cue always demanded a prompt recall; one that did not allow for any hesitation. Indeed, if the dog interrupted the recall for any reason, he was corrected or asked to repeat the exercise. In the formal *Drop on Recall* you are asking him to do precisely what you have taught him not to do in his previous training — to interrupt one command (the recall) and substitute another (the drop).

Fig. 7.5. Bear loves to play on the bed, responding to my commands to sit, stand, or lie down. I have worked hard to make this game intrinsically reinforcing to her.

This is confusing for most dogs because you are changing their previous understanding of the criteria for a successful recall. Many dogs respond to this confusion initially by doing at least one of the following: slowing down the recall, dropping reluctantly or incompletely, dropping on the recall cue itself, or refusing to do anything at all. While none of these behaviors is desirable, you would most emphatically not want to introduce aversives into the picture at this point. From the dog's point of view, changing the rules is aversive enough. Thus, even if the dog makes the slowest of movements toward you and only begins to drop on command, you will tell him he is on the right track! At the same time, you do not want to reward inappropriate behaviors such as moving forward during the drop. Since you should not correct during this learning phase, you will need to help. Therefore, you might position a broad jump board between yourself and the dog (but closer to the dog), and give the drop command just before the dog reaches the board. The board provides an additional cue to prevent the dog from moving forward after the command to drop, particularly if it was used earlier to help prevent forward motion on the stationary drop.

Don't worry if at this point the dog's recall and drop behaviors appear to have deteriorated radically. Whenever something new is introduced, behaviors that were previously flawless will deteriorate. Once the new element has been assimilated, the deteriorated behavior will correct itself. Your job is to do all you can to help the dog perform a reinforceable behavior with each new step. Although it may seem like you are taking two steps forward, one step back, in the long run it produces a dog who is not afraid to learn. New requests or a different environment are not a source of anxiety, but of increased opportunity for reinforcement.

Step 3. Progressing Toward the Formal Recall

This step is an easy one. Replace the board with a smaller board and then a dowel or leash. In addition, move the board or its equivalent to different places in the path of the recall so the dog does not learn to drop always at the same point. Next, introduce multiple boards so the dog gets used to coming over some boards before stopping behind another. Ultimately you will remove the boards, and the drop command will be the only stimulus the dog needs.

Although you can occasionally do a straight recall, you shouldn't do many of them. Don't try to fool your dog by making him believe that he will never be dropped in the ring. This is dishonest, and your dog needs to be able to trust you and his training. You should never ask him to do something in the ring he has not been thoroughly taught in training. In the long run, techniques like those increase the likelihood that the dog will either anticipate a drop in the ring or refuse to drop at all. It is important for the dog to know that he will be dropped in the ring. 'No surprises' should be everyone's training motto! To prevent the dog from anticipating the drop, you need to teach him the significance of each cue, not instill a false belief that one of the cues might never be given.

Proofing

Some trainers disapprove of proofing because they associate it with the use of aversives. This does not need to be the case. Proofing is nothing more than helping the dog to understand which stimuli are appropriate. The verbal or signaled cues are the only stimuli that should invoke the dog's response. You want the dog to ignore all aspects of the environment except you and your commands. In proofing, you introduce a variety of environmental variables and teach your dog to ignore them. Unless you have a dog that has a strong innate desire to focus solely on you, you need to teach your dog what to ignore in the environment and what to observe.

There is no such thing as an absolute understanding of an exercise. A dog's understanding changes as the context changes. In the initial stages of proofing, you help the dog do the exercise correctly. If he makes a mistake and responds to an inappropriate environmental cue, you might simply insist that he perform the exercise again, or you might back up and make performance easier for him. Your ultimate goal is to make it clear to the dog that he must obey your commands regardless of distractions.

Aversives

There are some occasions when aversives are advisable. Dogs that are not corrected on any part of the exercise, or are not corrected until they are asked to offer the full behavior in new or distracting environments, may come to associate the new environment with aversive stimuli. As a result, they may be frightened by changes in the environment. These are the dogs who perform beautifully in their own backyards but who fall apart as soon as they set foot on the show grounds.

If you intend to do any proofing that requires the use of aversives, it is best to introduce aversives early and in familiar places. Proofing should be introduced as a kind of game. By saying cheerfully, "Let's see how quickly you can drop. Oh, surely you can drop faster than that," and accompanying that by a light tap on the head or shoulder, you can introduce an aversive in a motivational and informative way. As long as you treat a slow drop as a challenge to do better and not a mistake to be corrected, your dog will accept proofing as nothing more than an interesting variation in the training game.

As the dog becomes more proficient at the proofing game, he is also learning the importance of not giving up, and the rewards inherent in trying harder. Begin your proofing in a familiar environment, and concentrate on a simple problem. For example, you might ask the dog to drop several times in the course of one recall or to drop on wet grass or cold concrete. If he refuses to even try to drop, you should apply an aversive and immediately help him to do the right thing. For instance, if your dog refuses even to pause on a drop command because of a distraction (after he has been taught to ignore distractions), you might take him back to the point at which he heard the command

and use his collar to force him into the down position. Then you might make the distraction a bit milder and praise enthusiastically for a better job.

Remember, when you introduce an aversive you must be sure that the dog has been taught how to prevent or escape it. Frightened or confused dogs are unable to learn. Dogs that are secure and not overwhelmed by too many different events are far more able to absorb the information. They can understand that the cause of the aversive is their own behavior rather than something in an unfamiliar environment.

Decide at the beginning of each training session which behaviors you will not tolerate and what you will do if those behaviors are offered. It is, after all, only fair to inform your dog about what is not allowed as well as what is going to be rewarded. For example, let's say that you are in the early stages of teaching the dog to fold back into a drop. Although the dog has already been taught to stand and stay, he insists on lunging forward as the food is presented rather than lowering his head to follow the food. It is perfectly reasonable and most informative for you to take him by the collar and push him back and down as the food is presented. This is aversive! Being pushed back and down is physical compulsion intended to cause mild discomfort for a dog who wants to move up and forward. But the compulsion is also coupled with the presentation of an appetitive — the food held between the dog's front legs. This serves to remind the dog of the desired behavior. You are saying to your dog, "Don't do this — do *this*." He learns to avoid the physical push back and down, and he learns to get the goodie by doing the drop. This is an aversive delivered early in the learning stage, in a familiar environment, in a calm and informative way. Not only does the dog learn to offer a specific behavior, he gains valuable information about the nature of aversives and how to avoid them.

Draw up a list of undesirable *Drop on Recall* behaviors and how you plan to respond to them if they happen. Do this before you encounter the behavior in a training session. The list won't be permanent — it will change as the dog's behaviors become more sophisticated and his own individual quirks emerge. However, you will have some idea of what you want and don't want. In the beginning, you may not want the dog to move forward during or after the drop, to drop from a sit (i.e., to sit first then lie down), to roll over on one hip, or to lunge for food. Although you do want him to drop promptly on command, you are not going to penalize him for anticipating the command at this stage in the learning process.

As you decide which behaviors you will not tolerate, you should also decide what aversives you will apply to inform the dog that these behaviors are not permitted. Aversives should be very mild in the beginning stages, and you should be ready to immediately show the dog how to escape them. For example, if he rolls on a hip after he drops, you could say, "Oops! Let's try that again," and release him upwards without any positive reinforcement. If he did the same thing on the next drop command, you might give the conditioned negative reinforcer, "Ahh, ahh," and pop him up into a stand or run backwards with him following you for a recall. A dog rolled on a hip cannot jump quickly up to avoid a pop, so this gives him a reason for not being on one hip. Of course, if the dog drops correctly, he will be asked to jump up for a treat — another reason for the correct drop.

The Payoff

Just as you will progressively ask for more in terms of behaviors, you should also be willing to give more in terms of reinforcements. If your dog gives you a super drop, you should have some extra special treats or toys to solidify that performance. Substitute quality for frequency of reinforcement. Use yourself increasingly as a primary reinforcer by playing games or initiating physical contact. Treat the entire drop exercise in such a way that it becomes a chain of behaviors with the opportunity to come in to you on the second part of the recall as the final payoff. Teach your dog that the faster he drops, the faster he will get to do wonderful things with you. Of course, if he doesn't drop at all, then he won't have any chance to get to you — he will be heeled back to the starting place to begin the whole chain again.

Ring Transitions

Gear your training toward the ultimate goal of competing. Expose your dog to the performance experience before the formal competition. Use matches to provide new environments. Don't wait until your dog is perfect to ask him to do the *Drop on Recall* in a ring environment. He needs to become comfortable in the ring and ultimately to perceive that environment as a friendly one. Make his first exposures positive — treat them no differently than you would his first trip to the park or training building. Use treats, toys, and games and, most of all, help him to perform correctly. As your dog becomes more familiar with the ring, you should gradually wean him off of all

159

reinforcements other than yourself. You should also try to limit your use of aversives. The performance ring is not the place for harsh corrections. Your dog needs to be able to work for you and for himself and for the enjoyment of the exercises.

Don't enter a competition until your dog can offer a reinforcement-free routine in a distraction-filled environment (Fig. 7.6). He does not have to be perfect, but he does have to be enthusiastic, willing, and happy. If there are signs of confusion or stress other than the excitement of the performance itself, break off the exercise and work on the problem outside of the ring. Don't teach him that if he offers less than satisfactory behaviors in the ring, food will reappear to refresh his memory.

In the week before the show, take your dog to a different place each day and perform only one *Drop on Recall*. Increase the positive reinforcement and minimize or totally eliminate aversives. Dogs frequently seem to develop total amnesia the day before a show. If you give in to preshow jitters and correct the dog harshly, you are setting your dog up for an unpleasant experi-ence — one that might create negative associations that last far beyond what-ever brief time you actually spend in the ring. If he forgets one aspect of the exercise, go back and show him how to do it, and reinforce that. If you've done your job correctly, that behavior *will* be there in the ring!

This entire process is a spiral gradually moving from less to more complicated behaviors, from familiar to unfamiliar environments, from con-stant reinforcement to random reinforcement to no reinforcement other than that which you can legally offer in the ring. A training program does not take a complete exercise all at once from the backyard to the park to the ring, but rather moves some parts of each exercise and corresponding reinforcements from location to location as the dog shows the trainer that he is growing more comfortable with the exercises and the environment. Once the environment ceases to be a factor in performance, you can increase the performance criteria necessary for reinforcement.

After the exercises have been polished and have been satisfactorily performed in the ring, you must try to keep them fun in practice. Regardless of how perfect your last performance was, do not limit your training sessions to routine run-throughs. Make a point of challenging your dog. Find ways to make individual exercises more difficult without making them threatening. Boredom is a great demotivator for both trainer and dog. It's your job to always make obedience fun for the team! When that happens, you and your dog will be a team that is competitive in every sense of the word, regardless of scores or titles.

Fig. 7.6. Once your dog is performing well without reinforcement in the presence of distractions, it's time to go to the Big Show!

Epilogue — You and Your Dog

Ultimately, you are the best positive reinforcer. All of the other positive reinforcers you use in training should bring the dog's focus and attention back to you. We are very fortunate as dog trainers because we are working with a species with which we have the opportunity to develop a deep and continuous relationship. We are training animals that have a long history of working for and with humans. Training a dog is not like training a marine mammal; it has the potential to be far more enriching. Although we cannot take treats into the ring with us the way the whale trainers take buckets of fish, neither can Sea World trainers take their animals home at night. This means that marine mammal trainers and their animals cannot develop the same degree of mutual pleasure that dogs and their owners derive from each other's company. In addition, dogs, unlike marine mammals, are domesticated — they have been selectively bred over centuries to live and work in the company of humans, to be members of a partnership with us. There is a reason they are called 'man's best friend.'

All canine performance events revolve around teamwork. Neither member of the human-canine team can perform alone. The very reason we do obedience, agility, hunting, or herding is because dog and handler take pleasure in their team work, or they ought to. Performance events are not business ventures for most of us. Our livelihood does not depend upon the color of the ribbon an amateur judge gives us. Togetherness and teamwork are the reasons that most of us compete. Togetherness should be the goal of every positive reinforcement that we give.

I have seen seminar hosts throw food that was intended to be positively reinforcing on the floor for the dog to eat. I have seen trainers use food as a substitute for physical contact with the dog. I also see good dog trainers play games with dogs that teach them to be other-directed. Games of fetch, for example, really excite the dog's prey or chase instincts. They direct the dog away from the trainer who often becomes just a device for putting the ball in motion. Far better to play tug with the toy when the dog brings it back, or to give the dog a better toy when he retrieves the item. It is crucial that you teach your dog that you are the source of reinforcement, and that working with you is the most wonderful thing in the world. That relationship is something you can take into the ring — something you can take home with you.

And if you and your dog have that — who needs money in the bank?

Training dogs gives us the opportunity to develop deep and continuous relationships with another species. Make sure that you are your dog's best reinforcer.

164

INDEX

V

Voice
   as a reinforcer 51
Voluntary behavior 16

W

Watch exercise 28